D0141474

GAYLORD R

THE BOOK OF MARMALADE

ITS ANTECEDENTS,
ITS HISTORY
AND ITS ROLE
IN THE WORLD TODAY

TOGETHER WITH
A COLLECTION OF
RECIPES FOR MARMALADES
and
MARMALADE COOKERY

REVISED EDITION

C. ANNE WILSON

University of Pennsylvania Press
Philadelphia
1999

Originally published 1985
Revised edition first published 1999 by Prospect Books
First published in the United States 1999 by University of Pennsylvania Press
Copyright © 1985, 1999 C. Anne Wilson
Printed on acid-free paper

10 9 8 7 6 5 4 3 2 1

641.852
W

Published by
University of Pennsylvania Press
Philadelphia, Pennsylvania 19104-4011

ISBN 0-8122-1727-6

Library of Congress Cataloging-In-Publication Data: available from the
Library of Congress

Printed in Great Britain.

For
M.C.W. & E.C.W.

TABLE OF CONTENTS

ILLUSTRATIONS

Quince tree. J. Gerard, *The Herball*, 1597.

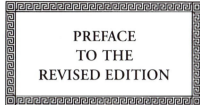

Marmalade continues to be newsworthy, whether through the new varieties introduced by enterprising manufacturers, or on account of National Marmalade Day, launched on 10 March 1995. The date celebrated the five hundredth anniversary of the earliest port record of the arrival of Portuguese marmalade in Britain, at the Port of London on 10 March 1495 (it had probably been coming in for some time already in small quantities, unnoticed by the customs men). The BBC Today Programme included a feature on the 1995 anniversary date, following an earlier suggestion by Brian Redhead; sadly, he did not live to share in that marmalade celebration. Since then, Chivers Hartley and Duerr's have supported National Marmalade Day on 10 March, giving it publicity in various ways.

The Frank Cooper company opened a marmalade shop and museum in 1985, close to the founder's original shop in the High Street, Oxford; and it thrived there for several years, though it no longer exists today. Duerr's have expanded year on year, and they place particular emphasis on their marmalades. Their advertising campaign in 1997 included the ingenious idea of a forty-foot-high hoarding on a particularly congested stretch of the M6 motorway bearing the words: 'Duerr's marmalades beat M6 jams'. Marmalade has had its successes in other English-speaking countries, too: Cottee's of Melbourne, Australia, have been expanding their production all through the 1990s. Most British firms also report expansion over the period, at least in sales of their 'premium brand' marmalades.

For the second edition of *The Book of Marmalade* I have rewritten large parts of Chapter VII and smaller sections elsewhere to bring the record up to date. As before, useful facts and figures have been supplied by the marmalade-making firms, and I would like to acknowledge the help of their representatives. My thanks go also to Susan Chesters and Helen Peacocke for assistance in tracking down elusive information. I hope marmalade-lovers everywhere will enjoy reading about this historic preserve.

C.A.W.

Leeds

June 1999

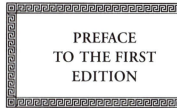

PREFACE TO THE FIRST EDITION

Every few years in the correspondence columns of *The Times* the argument about marmalade is resumed. Its champions write in to say it was invented by Janet Keiller, by Mary, Queen of Scots, by the Portuguese, and they cite erudite works telling about the uses to which it was put. It seems almost unsporting to produce a book which will settle the argument once for all. But the long, complicated story of marmalade and its antecedents has fascinated me for some time, and now I have succumbed to the temptation to write it out and share it.

When the publishers asked to have the story brought up to date with information on marmalade's place in the world today, I had the chance to delve into its very recent history, and realised that this is an ongoing affair, and that new fashions in marmalade are continuing to emerge, not only in Britain, but in English-speaking countries overseas. In some ways the wheel has come full circle. Marmalade was a very special gift in the reign of King Henry VIII. In the 1980s the 'premium sector', supplying expensive marmalades intended for the food-gift market, is the most buoyant part of the marmalade trade. But whereas we once imported our marmalade from Portugal, Spain and Italy, now we send it as an export all over the world.

Many friends and colleagues have been kind enough to contribute facts or recipes, or both, to this study. I should like to express special thanks to Dr Wendy Childs, Alan and Jane Davidson, Professor Constance Hieatt, Janet Hine, Helen Peacocke, Jennifer Stead,

Rosemary Suttill, and Beth Tupper. My thanks are due also to the following firms and their representatives, who sent me useful material on several aspects of marmalade manufacture: Baxters (Mr W. M. Biggart), Chivers (Miss E. Greenwood), Frank Cooper (Mrs C. Hooper), Crosse & Blackwell (Mr R. H. Starling), Elsenham (Mr A. J. G. Blunt and Ms G. Sinclair), Fortnum & Mason (Mr K. Hansen), Keiller (Mr C. H. Blakeman), Robertson (Ms J. Meek), and Wilkin of Tiptree (Mr I. K. Thurgood).

Most of the older recipe books consulted are among those in the Blanche Leigh and John F. Preston collections of early cookery-books in the Brotherton Library at the University of Leeds. Nearly all cookery-books from Elizabethan times onwards contain marmalade recipes, but the ones listed in the bibliography are the books and the editions which were used in compiling the present text. Individual page numbers have not been cited, as most of the books have indexes, so the keen marmalade-sleuth can find the recipes without difficulty in contemporary copies of the books, or in modern facsimile reprints.

Twenty-one of the most significant early recipes are printed in full in a separate section on historical recipes (pp. 145–153). The modern recipes which follow are divided into two sections, one for marmalades, and the other for a wide range of meat dishes, sauces, puddings, cakes, pastries, etc. in which marmalade is an ingredient.

Preparing this book has been a pleasant and interesting task, and I hope it will give pleasure to its readers.

C.A.W.
Leeds
May 1984

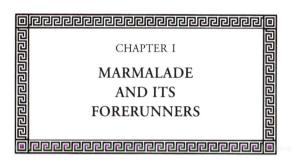

CHAPTER I

MARMALADE
AND ITS
FORERUNNERS

MARMALADE AND ITS NAME

Marmalade spread generously upon slices of freshly-made buttered toast: this, we like to believe, is the traditional English ending to the traditional English breakfast. Some would go further, and insist that the original home of the marmalade tradition was Scotland, and that it reached the English from their Scottish neighbours. Yet there is something strange about the name of this confection. Why should it derive from the Portuguese *marmelo,* meaning quince, when traditional British marmalade is made from Seville oranges (with such alternatives as lime, grapefruit, lemon or ginger marmalade generally regarded as more recent variations on the primary theme of bitter orange)?

And is marmalade unique to Britain? Its name is certainly not confined to the English language. When we travel abroad we find that in nearly every country of Europe people have the term 'marmalade' in their vocabulary – spelled sometimes rather strangely to our eyes, but clearly the same word. Moreover, it is often applied to a much wider range of conserves there than it is in Britain. One reason is that non-English-speaking nations lack an exact equivalent for our 'jam'.

This leads to some interesting comparisons. Holiday-makers in Greece will receive on their hotel breakfast tables, along with the bread and rusks (and often pieces of cake, a nostalgic reminder of bygone times, for in the eighteenth century we too, in Britain, ate cake for breakfast), pats of butter and little pots of conserve covered with foil. Upon the foil will be the name in Greek characters, MARMELADA PHRAOULA, and beneath that the English translation, STRAWBERRY JAM. On other days the contents of the pots will differ, and the translations will read, QUINCE JAM, APRICOT JAM, GRAPE-FRUIT JAM, ORANGE JAM, and so on. In every case, the Greek term will be MARMELADA, plus the name of the fruit.

In Italy, likewise, MARMELLATA is made of peaches, or apricots, or figs (fig *marmellata* is an Italian speciality) or greengages, or apples, or pears; while orange marmalade has to be defined as MAR-MELLATA DI ARANCE AMARE (bitter oranges), or DI AGRUMI (citrus fruits). French MARMALADE is defined in Littré's dictionary as fruit cooked with sugar for so long that skin and flesh are completely melded together to form a single substance of uniform consistency. The idea is extended to other foods which are cooked until they turn into a sticky, homogeneous mass, when they are described as being '*en marmelade*'. In Germany and the Scandinavian countries, marmalades may be of any fruits, and if they are made of oranges or lemons, then the names of those fruits must be added to the word MARMELADE or its equivalent.

The British themselves have not always had their soft-fruit jams. The word 'jam' began to creep into manuscript cookery-books in the last quarter of the seventeenth century, and into the printed ones early in the eighteenth. It had entered the English language only about a hundred years before; and perhaps it had a middle-eastern origin, for there is an Arab word '*jam*' which means 'close-packed' or 'all together'. From its more general usage in English for things that were jammed against one another, the word passed into the realm of confectionery, to denote those preserves where soft fruits cooked with sugar were crushed together, rather than sieved, and could thus truly be described as 'jammed', or 'in a jam'.

Still earlier, the soft fruits were sometimes boiled down with sugar to a very thick and solid consistency which had the name 'marmalade' joined to that of the fruit, for instance, 'drie marmalade of peaches' in A.W.'s *A Book of Cookrye,* 1587, and 'marmalade of damsons or prunes' in John Partridge's *The Treasurie of Commodious Conceites,* 1584. But at that time, and indeed until well into the eighteenth century, the word 'marmalade' used by itself meant only one thing: marmalade of quinces. And here we can begin to see the possibility of a link with Portuguese quinces.

In Tudor times, well-to-do English families enjoyed a number of luxury foods imported from southern Europe, including sugar and sugar-candy, oranges, lemons, dried fruits and sweet wines. So when the Portuguese traders set off with their figs, raisins and citrus fruits, oil, wax and honey, in the holds of their galleys, they could well have found it profitable sometimes to add a small stock of a local conserve confected from quinces and sugar, and called in Portuguese *marmelada* because it was made from the *marmelo,* or quince.

In fact, marmalade did first arrive thus in England from Portugal, and before long also from Spain and Italy, where the Portuguese term for the confection was likewise adopted. The earliest English references to marmalade are therefore to be found in port records, where the names of the shipper and his ship and the value of its cargo were set down, so that appropriate duties could be charged. But before long English travellers to Mediterranean lands began to bring back recipes for this delectable sweetmeat; and then marmalade could be made in England too, from home-grown quinces and imported sugar, which was rather less costly than the versions which arrived by sea from southern Europe.

MELOMELI AND CIDONITUM: THE ANCIENT WORLD

The origins of quince marmalade are to be traced back far beyond the sixteenth century, and its very recognisable forebears can be identified in the home-made preserves of Roman times, and in the recipes of the Greek physicians. The physicians valued the prepared quinces and quince jellies as aids to digestion, and recommended them for various complaints affecting the stomach, liver and kidneys. But the methods whereby the quinces were conserved must have been invented originally because people wanted to enjoy some part of their fruit crops through the winter and spring months.

The earliest system of fruit preservation was probably based upon drying; there is evidence that apples were cut up and dried in slices in Neolithic Britain.[1] But in time other alternatives were discovered. When Cato wrote about work on the farm in Italy in the second century BC, he advised the wife of the bailiff to keep 'a large store of dried pears, sorbs (fruit of the service tree, related to the rowan), figs, raisins...(and) preserved pears and grapes and quinces. She should also have grapes preserved in grape-pulp, and Scantian quinces kept in jars.' Apuleius, three centuries later, gave further advice, which has been transmitted in Book I of Apicius' cookery-book. Grapes were to be put in a little boiled water within sealed jars made airtight with pitch, or were to be stored dry in barley; mulberries were to be kept in mulberry-juice mixed with *sapa* (wine-must boiled down and reduced to a syrup). As for quinces, 'Choose faultless quinces with their twigs and leaves, and put them in a receptacle, and pour over honey and *defrutum* [wine-must reduced to an even thicker consistency than *sapa*]; *you* will keep them for a long time.'[2]

So quinces could be preserved successfully in a state of completeness. But already another mode of preservation had been devised for them. According to the recipe of Dioscorides, the first-century AD physician, quinces, peeled and with their pips removed, were wedged together as tightly as possible in honey in a vessel. After a year they became as soft as 'wine-honey', a preparation for which wine and honey were boiled together and reduced to a thick consistency. [See R 1.] This method was a Greek invention, and its Greek name, *mēlomeli* (apple-in-honey), passed into Latin as the *melomeli* of Columella, and the *melimela* (honey-apples, with an implied inversion of the two parts of the word) of Martial. From this word the Portuguese eventually derived their word for quince, *marmelo,* and hence their *marmelada.*

Dioscorides' apples-in-honey were uncooked, relying on long storage and the weight of the close-packed fruit to make them soft and sweet, and no doubt they were eaten still sticky from the honey. Columella's version did not even require the cores and pips to be removed from the quinces, nor were they packed tightly in the honey which alone served to check corruption, and prevent its spread. But Pliny stressed that the air should be excluded in order to keep quinces; and said they should either be cooked in honey or submerged in it, which suggests that a cooked form of *melomeli* was also known. Columella warned that unripe quinces stored in honey became too hard to be any use, which shows the reason why some quinces were cooked in the honey prior to storage. Preserved quinces were sweet, but apparently tasted somewhat insipid, for Martial wrote of children being given *melimela* and also large, sweet, but inferior, figs, and he contrasted his own adult preference for Chian figs with a good strong flavour.[3]

The Greek name for quinces was Cydonian apples *(mēla Kudōnia),* because it was said that the finest ones came from Cydonia, a city in north-west Crete. It was not the original home of the quince; that lay further north and east, probably in those parts of western Asia where the trees still grow wild today. The term *mēlomeli* incorporated the 'apple' section of the Greek name together with *meli,* meaning honey. But the Latin word for quinces, *cotonea,* came directly from the other section, *Kudōnia;* and by various mutations it produced medieval French *coin,* and our 'quince' (originally a plural form of an obsolete word *quine,* which must represent the English attempt to spell *coin* as pronounced in Anglo-Norman French).

It also produced the name of a second form of quince preserve, *kudōnitēs* in Greek, *cydonitum* or *cidonitum* in Latin. This word, too, was destined to re-emerge much later as the 'quidony of quinces' of Tudor and Stuart times. In Dioscorides' Greek recipe, *kudōnitēs* can be made in two ways, either by cutting up the quinces like turnips, steeping them in sweet wine-must for 30 days, then straining off the liquid (which must have become thick and jellyish from the pectin in the quinces); or by pressing out the juice as soon as the quinces had been cut up, and mixing it with honey in the ratio of twelve parts of juice to one of honey. It was good for the stomach, and for those with dysentery and liver and kidney complaints.

But the recipes for *cidonitum* given by Palladius in the fourth century AD, which have the quinces peeled, cut up and boiled in honey, or alternatively their juice extracted, mixed with vinegar and honey, and cooked to the consistency of honey, also have a further notable addition. Pepper was shaken into both types of *cidonitum,* and into the second one, ginger as well.[4] [See R 2.] It is clear that others beside Martial had found *melimela* and unseasoned *cidonitum* insipid.

The addition of pepper is not surprising. Nearly all the sweet dishes in Apicius' cookery book, based on various combinations of nuts and honey, eggs and milk, are sprinkled with pepper before they are served. The Romans took special pleasure in the pungency of pepper in any bland dish, whether sweet or otherwise. It was their favourite spice, with ginger the second most-liked.

It was the spiced *cidonitum* that was to survive into medieval times in western Europe. It may have been handed down partly as a sweetmeat, but it was also recognised as a medicine, and was well suited to that role, because the spices which went into it could be varied according to the patient's needs. Paul of Aegina, a Greek physician of the earlier seventh century AD, offered recipes for two forms of quince preparation. One of them, said to be the recipe of Galen, used only the juice of quinces, seasoned with ginger and white pepper and boiled with honey and some ginger until it jelled. It was recommended as a cure for poor appetite, and also for indigestion. For the other one, the fruit was sliced and boiled in wine with honey and several spices, including pepper, parsley-seed, ginger, spikenard, and cloves, until the liquid jelled; the quince slices were left in the liquor as it cooled and set.[5]

These are the earliest recipes to mention the jelling *(sustasis)* of the quince preparations. Quinces have a high pectin content, and it was their pectin, reacting with the sugar in the honey and the acid in the wine or vinegar of these early recipes, which caused the juice to jell and set. This must raise the question: why only quinces? There were other pectin-rich fruits available in the ancient world: sharp apples, damsons, and certain types of plum. Were these never cooked and preserved in the same manner? The answer is that they apparently were not.

The most likely reason is that fruits selected by the Romans for preservation in honey would have been the finest and sweetest available; and they were submerged in the honey in their fresh, uncooked state. Quinces were exceptional because, if not totally ripe, they remained hard even in the honey, as Columella warned. It was to avoid this risk that the quinces were sometimes first cooked in wine and honey, and thus it came about that their pectin was activated, jelling their juice and turning them into a conserve, the basis for *cidonitum.* The high pectin content of some other sharp fruits may never have been discovered because there was no incentive to precook them in honey (wild plums and onyx-coloured plums were pickled in a mixture of wine-must and vinegar with salt, according to Columella).[6] So quinces remained unchallenged in the field of the pectin-jellied conserve.

CHARDEQUYNCE INTO MARMELADA: THE MEDIEVAL WORLD

Both *cidonitum* and *melomeli* made their mark in the medieval West, but in rather different ways. The spiced quince preserves of north-west Europe are known from their recipes, which do not differ in essential ingredients from Palladius' *cidonitum*. The *condoignac* in the *Ménagier de Paris,* a French household book of *c.*1394, is obviously a descendant. The versions in the English cookery-books are called *chardequynce,* which translates *cidonitum* very literally as 'flesh of quince'.

But *melomeli,* which Isidore of Seville (*c.*AD 570–636) called *malomellus,* had already acquired a second meaning in his day. He wrote, in his *Etymologies,* 'Malomellus is named from its sweetness, [either] because its fruit has the flavour of honey, or because it is preserved in honey.'[7] From this we can deduce that in seventh-century Spain the quince itself was already known as *malomellus,* though Isidore's words seem to imply that both the fruit and the conserve made from it may then have been called by this same name, just as both are called *membrillo* in Spain today. Thereafter the name in Spain passed through a series of changes, from *malomellus to* the Mozarabic *malmâlo,* to the Castilian *merimello,* and thence to *membrillo.* In the late middle ages, when *chardequynce* was appearing in English cookery and medical recipe books, the Spanish form was sometimes called *carne de membrillo* (flesh of membrillo).[8]

Meanwhile, in that region of the Iberian peninsula which eventually became Portugal, the local dialect went through a slightly different development as Mozarabic *malmâlo* became *marmelo,* the modern Portuguese word for a quince; and the form of quince conserve made there during the late middle ages acquired the name *marmelada.* The conserve had changed from those previously discussed in one important aspect: it was now sweetened not with honey, but with sugar.

Sugar was one magic ingredient destined to distinguish quince *marmelada,* and the *marmellata* and 'marmelet' which soon copied it elsewhere in Europe, from their honey-based predecessors. Sugar was a very suitable partner for quinces in a spiced, jellied conserve of a partly medicinal character, because sugar had itself begun its European career as a medicine. To us today it seems remarkable that the gourmets of imperial Rome did not discover culinary or preservative uses for the sugar that was imported along with oriental spices from India, for they took great delight in luxury foods from other distant places – oysters from Britain; sturgeon from the Black Sea.

Sugar had been known to the Mediterranean world from the time of Alexander's expedition to India (325 BC). His admiral Nearchos, returning with news of strange and marvellous things to be seen in that land, reported the presence there of 'reeds [which] produce honey, although there are no bees.' In the days of the Roman empire, sugar arrived in Rome together with pepper, ginger and other spices from India and lands still further east. But although Pliny knew it, and described it as a kind of honey collected from reeds and solidified into lumps the size of a hazelnut or smaller, and brittle to the teeth, he said that it was only used in medicine. Its medicinal properties were explained by Dioscorides: it was good for the stomach, the bowels, the kidneys and the bladder; and it was to be dissolved in water and taken in the form of a drink.[9]

The Persians may have been the earliest people to adopt sugar as a foodstuff. They certainly introduced sugar-canes into their territories, initially as medicinal plants. But the crop became more widespread, and well before the time of the Arab conquest, sugar was being cultivated in the Tigris and Euphrates delta, and in parts of Baluchistan. Honey had culinary uses as well as medicinal ones, and thus supplied a precedent for sugar, too, to become both a foodstuff and a preserving agent. It is very possible that when the Arabs occupied Persia, they encountered sugar already in use as a food, perhaps with dietary overtones, for sugar was moderately warming, according to the Galenic system of the four humours, and thus it was a useful addition to the diet of those with cold constitutions.

We have no contemporary Persian recipes to supply confirmation. But a few Arabic ones survive, belonging to the tenth century and to the court circle of the Baghdad caliphs of the Abbasid dynasty, which looked back to older Persian traditions in many cultural spheres. These recipes show that sugar was used to make 'lozenge', a confection of ground almonds, breadcrumbs, sesame-oil, rosewater, and sugar; and to sweeten delicious dishes of rice, either white and shining by itself, or cooked in chicken-fat and made golden with saffron.[10] The later cookery and medical books of the Arabs indicate continuing use of sugar to prepare sweet dishes, and to make fruit syrups and conserves. It is easy to see how much they valued sugar, and why they spread its cultivation westwards in the wake of their conquests, to Egypt, North Africa, and the larger Mediterranean islands.

Medieval Arab recipes for quinces preserved with honey or sugar still exist, but remain untranslated. There is a tantalising reference to such a recipe in Professor M. Rodinson's French summary of the thirteenth-century *Wuṣla ilā l'habīb,* where 'quince cooked with sugar' is a heading in the section on fruit syrups and electuaries (semi-solid syrups, originally honey-based), which were items similarly confected with sugar.[11] There is as yet no western language translation of this book, and the much-abridged Baghdad cookery-book of 1226 in the English version of A. J. Arberry contains no recipe for sugar-preserved quinces. But in the sixteenth century it was said that the Moors of North Africa had taught the Portuguese to gobble up *marmelada.*[12] So it does look as though Arab food customs and recipes were the original source of this confection in Portugal; and hence in the other western European countries which adopted it.

In the meantime, the Christian West had not been without quince preserves. In France, *cidonitum* became *condoignac*. Its recipe, in the Parisian household book written for a young bride about 1394, has the quinces peeled and cored, cooked first in red wine and then in honey, and eventually well spiced, cooled, cut up into pieces and stored. [See R 3.] In a fifteenth-century Venetian recipe, *codigniato is* made with quinces, honey and fine spices; the spices may be replaced by six ounces of sugar for every three pounds of *codigniato*. [13]

Most of the surviving English recipes for chardequynce belong to the fifteenth century. They follow the French *condoignac* in their general form, with a preliminary cooking of the quinces in ale-wort rather than wine, followed by the sieving of the pulp, the recooking in honey, and the spicing with pepper, ginger, and cinnamon or galingale. A new feature is the addition of ten warden pears to thirty quinces, to form the fruit component; for it had been found that the quinces could carry the extra pears, although they were poorer in pectin, and still yield a solid jelly that could be cut up, boxed and stored. For chardequynce was always stored in boxes. Recipes are to be found both in cookery-books and in collections of medical remedies, and they no doubt appeared in the West first of all in medical books, copied there from the texts of the Greek physicians. The recipe in one cookery-book (MS Harleian 4016) of *c.*1450 concludes its instructions for making chardequynce with the words, 'And it is comfortable for a man's body, and namely for the stomach.'[14]

Chardequynce was eaten at the end of a medieval feast or sub-stantial dinner, when it was offered along with pears, nuts, sugar-coated aniseed or caraway comfits, white and green ginger, and 'composts' (fruits and nuts preserved in a honey and vinegar pickle). The purpose of all the foods in this group was 'your stomach for to ease';[15] and it is clear that the spiced quince preserve had kept this role from the days of Dioscorides and Galen.

By the fifteenth century, the usages of chardequynce were being extended. It became an ingredient in cookery. A special version of the pottage called 'mawmeny', made from shredded capons' or pheasants' flesh, cooked in wine, thickened with rice-flour, and enriched with sugar, currants, sliced ginger, and spices, had the further addition of half a pound of 'paste royal' (a kind of marzipan) and half a pound of chardequynce. This pottage was almost a fore-runner of our Christmas pudding, for when it had been spooned out into bowls, it was topped with aqua vitae, set alight with a candle, 'and serve it forth burning'.[16]

In the same period, the spiced chardequynce began to be made with sugar in place of honey. That led to its being treated sometimes in the manner of other pastes of worked sugar which were exploited for decorative purposes. The quince paste could be set into shapes in oiled moulds and, according to one recipe, the shapes were then gilded or silvered with foil applied by means of white of egg, or dyed red with brazil-wood, or blue with indigo or woad. The same recipe explains a method for storing quince-pulp by boiling it up with sugar (three pounds of pulp to one of sugar) 'till they wax somewhat stiff on a knife-point, and then put it in a fair pot, and so ye may keep it as long as ye will from year to year.' When re-quired, it could be worked up into chardequynce by reboiling the stiffened pulp with an equal quantity of sugar. [17]

The changeover from honey to sugar as an active ingredient of chardequynce is recorded in a group of three recipes from a leech-book of about 1444. The first is the traditional chardequynce of quinces and warden pears, honey, and spices, and it carries the comment: 'This manner of making is good, and if it is thus made, it will be black.' The second is said to be better, because the fruit is precooked in water only, not in ale-wort, and a mixture of two parts of honey to three of sugar is substituted for honey alone. But the third is 'the best of all', for it is made simply from equal weights of purified sugar and quinces, without pears, or honey, 'and this shall be whiter than that other, inasmuch as the sugar is white, [so] shall the chardequynce be.' [See R 4.]

At that point, chardequynce had begun to approach very close to the quince and sugar *marmelada* of the Portuguese. Possibly the English actually learned to make chardequynce with sugar through the influence of the Portuguese version of the sweetmeat. Portuguese *marmelada* may occasionally have been brought to England as early as the first half of the fifteenth century without leaving any written record of its presence; or travellers and traders who encountered it in Portugal or Spain may at least have been able to bring back the secret of its manufacture.

But the foreign *marmelada* of southern Europe continued to be regarded as a novelty in England through much of the sixteenth century, and the reason must have been more than just its sugar content. Its Arab origins have already been hinted at, and we may suspect that the Portuguese quince and sugar confection was delicately flavoured with the rosewater so beloved in Arab cookery and adopted into the partly Moorish cuisine of medieval Spain and Portugal; and possibly also with a soupçon of another perfume. This theory is borne out by the presence of rosewater in the earliest English marmalade recipes we know, those in the printed books of Elizabeth I's reign, which may be assumed to have come directly from southern European originals. Musk and rosewater occur together in some recipes, such as the one given by Gerard in his *Herball* of 1597.[18] A century later, rosewater was still the characteristic flavouring for quince marmalade in Spain. A recipe published in W. Salmon's *The Family Dictionary* in 1696 for 'Marmalade the Spanish way' shows rosewater added twice to the quince preserve during the cooking process; and there is a final instruction to 'Strew over some perfumed comfits, and keep it close for use.'

One of the first marmalade recipes to be published in English was in the translated version of *The Secrets of Alexis of Piedmont*,

1562 (from the original Italian of 1557 via the French translation). Here, though no rosewater is mentioned, the marmalade of quince-pulp, boiled first alone and then with sugar, was to be flavoured, if desired, with musk. So as to allay any doubt that such was the current fashion in marmalade in southern Europe, the translator of the *Secrets* headed the recipe with a comprehensive summary of the situation: 'To make conserve or confiture of quinces, called in Latin Cotoneatum, Cydoniatum or Cidonites, as they do in Valence [Valencia, Spain], which also the Genoese do use, we call it in England marmalade.' He ended his recipe with the claim, 'Better marmalade of quinces, sweeter and heartier than this, a man cannot make.'[19]

The marmalade imported into England at that time came from Spain and Italy as well as from Portugal; so it may safely be deduced that it was the novel flavourings which distinguished that marmalade from its jellied-quince predecessor, chardequynce, and made it a new, fashionable conserve for the well-to-do. Interestingly, the recipe of Alexis of Piedmont offers the alternative possibility of adding cinnamon, cloves, nutmeg and ginger as the flavourings, 'if you will'. It thus stands as a bridge between the new food-scents, such as musk or rosewater, and the traditional spices of medieval chardequynce or French *condoignac*.

But the English soon lost interest in the old spiced form of the preserve (which hereafter appeared only in a few rather specialised recipes in the printed cookery-books). Henceforth their choice was for marmalade based on the southern European version, flavoured at first with rosewater or musk or both, but soon to be simplified to the two basic ingredients of quinces and sugar, without further seasoning.

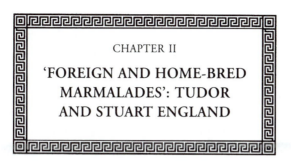

CHAPTER II

'FOREIGN AND HOME-BRED
MARMALADES': TUDOR
AND STUART ENGLAND

MARMELADO AND CODINIAC

Marmalade has made a striking first appearance in some history books because of an old tradition that the Anti-pope Peter de Luna, when he was confined in a castle on the islet of Peniscola off the east coast of Spain, almost lost his life in July 1418 through eating poisoned marmalade. It is sad to have to cast doubt on this dramatic event, but contemporary sources do not support it. They give another version, wherein Peter consumed not marmalade, but honey-filled wafers, well dosed with poison by his enemies; and afterwards some play was made on the contrast between the Holy Wafer of the Mass and the unholy wafers which transmitted their deadly filling to the Anti-pope. He survived this attempt on his life because the poison, probably arsenic, caused such violent vomiting that most of it was ejected from his system before it could prove fatal.[1]

The earliest evidence for marmalade is in reality more prosaic. It takes the form of records of imports of marmalade into England belonging to the time when it was beginning to arrive by sea in quantities large enough to have to be declared and valued at its port of entry, along with the rest of the ship's cargo. The earliest surviving records all refer to Portuguese ships and shippers, and thus confirm that the English received the word *marmelada* direct from Portugal, since it was from there that they first had the product itself. On 10 March 1495 '6 pec' [pieces] marmelad'' arrived at the Port of London in the ship of Farnando Yanes; on 26 March they were followed there, in a single day, by 40 lb. of marmalade on the ship of Peter Founse, and four further consignments, adding up to 45 lb. plus 3 'coffers', brought in by four different traders on the ship of Martin Yanus. The customs accounts of Exeter show that, on 17 January 1499, Peter Farnando landed from the ship *Rosary* of Oporto 60 lb. of marmalade valued at 20s. (£1).[2]

The quantities of marmalade which arrived in some of the early shipments are not always so clear. A 'little chest' *(parva cista)* of marmalade was delivered at Southampton during the year 1500–1. Between 10 October 1502 and 26 May 1503, 1 barrel, 1 pot, 3 little pots and 1 rove (a somewhat variable weight, often about 25 lb.) of marmalade entered the Port of London at various times. The ships and shippers were all Portuguese, except for Martin Colongas, on whose ship the above-mentioned barrel was conveyed, and he may have been a Basque.

The barrel was valued at 20s., but the other containers carried no valuation, being part of larger consignments of mixed goods, all taxed together. The figure of 20s. for the 60 lb. of marmalade brought into Exeter in 1499 shows that its wholesale price was 4d. (under 2p) a pound. The same costing is suggested by the entry in a book of rates issued in London in 1507. The *marmelado* here is in fact given the unlikely value of £4 a lb., but this must surely be due to miscopying in the eighteenth-century transcript of the book which has turned pence into £s (for comparison, succade, a confection of citrus fruit-peels in sugar syrup, also imported from southern Europe, was no more than 4d. a lb. on the same list).[3] The retail price is less certain, and there may have been a considerable write-up initially because of the novelty of the marmalade. When chardequynce was purchased for the household of George, Duke of Clarence, in 1469, ten one-pound boxes cost 5s. (25p) each; and the Portuguese marmalade may at first have sold for comparable sums.[4]

The price of marmalade fell in the following decades. By 1537 Lady Lisle's man was able to buy fine *marmelado* for her at 9d. (under 4p) a lb., after he had spurned the coarser quality, which was only 6d. (2 ¹/₂p) a lb., but was 'nothing worth'.[5] *Marmelado,* as this Spanish form of the name implies, was by then arriving from Spain and Italy, though the Portuguese connection continued. Marmalade, along with sugar-preserved fruits and candied peels, formed part of a consignment of sweetmeats which the 'factor of Portyugale' supplied to Thomas Cromwell in 1537.[6] Marmalade grew more expensive again in the inflationary years towards the end of the century. A household book for 1587–8 belonging to Lord Middleton of Wollaton Hall, Nottinghamshire, has an entry on 22 July for 2 lb. 1 oz. marmalade purchased for 5s. 3d. (26 ¹/₂p) along with 1 lb. of sucket at 2s. 6d. (12 ¹/₂p), so marmalade and sucket or succade at that time cost almost exactly the same.[7] But the price may well have fluctuated a good deal from season to season, according to the availability of the marmalade and its quality.

The marmalade which was offered for sale through this period was a sweet, solid quince jelly, flavoured with rosewater and musk, or occasionally other food scents. It could be used for purely medicinal purposes, but was also a delicious sweetmeat to be served at the end of a fine dinner or a special supper, just as chardequynce had been in former times. It was an attractive commodity; and as a result the marmalade named in the household accounts of a number of important Tudor figures was not always recorded there as a purchase; or, if it was so recorded, was not necessarily intended for the person on whose behalf it had been bought. Marmalade was a very acceptable gift, one that could be offered in the sure knowledge that it would cause the recipient to look with favour upon the donor. Not surprisingly, in one of the earliest records of a gift of marmalade, the recipient was no less a person than King Henry

VIII. His Letters and Papers for 1524 supply the information: 'Presented by Hull of Exeter, one box of marmalade'.[8]

Lady Lisle both gave and received marmalade at various times during the 1530s. In a letter to Lord Lisle on 12 May 1534, William Grett wrote, 'I have sent unto your lordship a box of marmaladoo, and another unto my good lady your wife'; while Richard Lee's letter to Lord Lisle, written on 14 December 1536, included the message: 'He most heartily thanketh her ladyship for her marmalado'.[9] While in France, Lady Lisle sent the French equivalent, *codiniac*, to at least three French friends, who acknowledged it gratefully, and also to King Henry VIII himself, for she was ever anxious that she, and still more her husband, should stand well in the royal favour. The king was much taken with it, and on 22 December 1539 Lady Lisle received a message from him requesting more 'of the codiniac of the clearest making and of the conserve of damsons'.[10]

In France quince preserve still went under its old medieval name much of the time, even though it was no longer made with its medieval seasoning of spices. More than a century after Lady Lisle sent her gift to the king, La Varenne gave French recipes for both clear *cotignac* and thick *cotignac;* and the latter, which included the pulp of the fruit, was very close to sixteenth- and seventeenth-century English recipes for quince marmalade. By contrast, La Varenne's 'marmalade de coings' is a runnier version of the thick *cotignac,* boiled for a shorter time, put up in faience pots, and presumably intended for more immediate consumption.[11]

MARMALADE AND QUIDONY

The difference between the clear jelly preserve and the thicker fruit-pulp version was recognised in England too. The clear form, set from the liquor filtered from the quinces, was at first called 'quodiniacke', but very soon became known as quidony or quiddany. The thicker conserve appeared in household books as 'marmalet', or 'marmulet' or other variants, before its name settled down as 'marmalade'. When it was prepared, the quinces underwent their two boilings, the first with water only, the second with sugar, and sometimes rosewater, musk or other perfume, and the conserve, at the point of jelling, was poured into boxes and left to set there. It could be turned out in one piece (hence the contemporary description of 'a brick of marmalade'), and when it was time to eat it, slices or chunks were cut from it, as is done with Spanish *membrillo* and the quince pastes sold in other southern European countries today.

But it was not always produced in brick-shaped boxes. One gift, presented to Sir William Petre of Ingatestone in 1549 by Sir Edward Dymoke, afterwards the royal champion, took the form of 'four boxes of marmelade small and a box of biscuit bread'.[12] This marmalade, divided into small sections, could have been imported marmalade from southern Europe. Alexis of Piedmont's authentic recipe for making it in the fashion of Valencia and Genoa advised spreading the cooked marmalade across a sugar-strewn table with a broad slice made of wood, 'and so make round, broad or long pieces, as you will, with the circle of a bore, of what greatness you liste; then set them in the sun until they be thorough dry.' The final instruction certainly sounds authentically southern European; in England, quince marmalade was home-made in October and November, when sunshine of marmalade-drying strength could hardly be guaranteed.

English chardequynce of the fifteenth century had sometimes been set in moulds, and this method of production also passed into marmalade-making. So Sir William Petre's 'marmelade small' may, after all, have been locally made, in small moulded shapes. The recipes emphasise the need to cook the confection to a solid consistency. 'Stir it till it be thick or stiff that your stick will stand upright of itself', said A.W.'s recipe of 1587. More usual was the injunction to drop a little of the boiling marmalade into a saucer, and test its density as it cooled. There were some problems in preventing it from sticking to the moulds as it set; and the 1587 recipe had the marmalade divided into 'pretty lumps' and cooled first, after which the lumps were well sugared and the moulds were fitted to them. [See R 5.] But later recipes always recommended wetting the moulds thoroughly with water or rosewater, and setting the marmalade in them direct. The moulds were shaped to represent fruits, or animals or birds, or occasionally household objects. They were made up of two or three interlocking pieces of wood, tin or alabaster (the wooden ones required a long pre-soaking in water if the marmalade was not to stick to them). When turned out, the moulded pieces of marmalade were left to stand in a cool oven after the bread had been drawn, or at a little distance from the fire (not in the sun in English recipes), until they were thoroughly dry and hard. Then they were boxed up.

Quince marmalade continued to be very popular, even though marmalades of other fruits were introduced. It was reliable to make because of the high pectin content of quinces, and it continued prominent in the cookery-books until late in the nineteenth century. One reason for its appeal to the Elizabethans and Jacobeans was the variations in colour that could be achieved when the quinces were cooked and combined with sugar in different ways. The numerous recipes for marmalade red, white or 'ordinary' (i.e. of a deep amber shade) show the amount of experimentation which went into achieving the right colour. [See R 6 and R 9.] The secret of the white was to use the whitest possible sugar (the earliest recipes explain how to clarify the sugar by boiling it in water to which frothed-up egg-whites were added, and removing the scum as it rose to the surface); and not to cook the mixture too long once the sugar had been added. Sir Hugh Plat suggested that the quince pulp, having been boiled and dried, should not be reboiled with sugar at all, but simply mixed with it: 'this marmalade will be white marmalade, and if you will have it look with an high colour, put your sugar and your pulp together, so soon as your pulp is drawn, and let them both boil together, and so it will look of the colour of ordinary marmalade, like unto a stewed warden [pear], but if you dry your pulp first, it will look white and take less sugar.'

Another method was put forward in *The Ladies Cabinet Opened*, published by Lord Patrick Ruthven in 1639: 'When you would preserve your quinces white, you must not cover them in the boiling, and you must put half as much sugar more for the white as for the other. When you would have them red, you must cover them in the boiling.' This book also identified the pectin-rich jelly around the quince seeds as a reliable setting agent, and advised that it be washed off 'in fair water, then strain the watered jelly from the kernels through some fine cobweb lawn, but put not so much into your [preserved] quinces as into the marmalade, for it will jelly the syrup too much.'

Many more recipes were published in the seventeenth century cookery and preserving handbooks, and ladies also initiated one another into the secrets of marmalade-making in the home. Samuel Pepys, on 2 November 1663, 'left Mrs Hunt and my wife making marmalett of quinces.' On 4 November he was able to report, 'Home to dinner and very pleasant with my wife who is this day also herself making of Marmalett of Quince, which she now doth very well herself. I left her at it …'[13]

Quidony, made from the same ingredients as marmalade, corresponded to the clear *cotignac* of France. The recipe required the quinces to be pared, cored and boiled for a time in a little water; the liquor was then strained off and reboiled with sugar, when it would set firmly. The leftover pulp could be added to pies or used up elsewhere. If the liquid was simply allowed to drip through the jelly-bag (usually a linen bag), the quidony was clear; but some people preferred to squeeze and wring every last drop from the bag, and then the quidony was still a jelly, but a cloudy one. It was boxed up like marmalade, or else set in moulds. Sir Hugh Plat's recipe for 'Quidini of Quinces', flavoured with rosewater, used only the kernels of the fruit, in which the pectin is stored. The liquor was boiled 'till you see it come to be of a deep colour: then take a drop and drop it on the bottom of a saucer, and if it stands, take it off, then let it run through a gelly bag into a bason, then set your bason upon a chafingdish of coals [a portable brazier heated by charcoal] to keep it warm, then take a spoon, and fill your boxes as full as you please, and when they be cold, cover them.'

The best white marmalade of quinces, later 17th century.
Brotherton Library, University of Leeds, MS 687, No. 47.
(See also R 9.)

MARMALADE AMONG THE 'BANQUETTING STUFFE'

An early glimpse of marmalade on a menu is given in the account of the foods served at the various 'boards' at the great feast which followed William Warham's enthronement as Archbishop of Canterbury on 9 March 1505. The Archbishop's lord steward and other lords 'sitting at a board at night' received two fish dishes, quince and orange pies, a tart, leche Florentine (a thick custard, sliced), marmalade, succade and comfits and wafers with their spiced wine.[14]

Marmalade was often served alongside succade during the sixteenth century. Perhaps they were frequently named together because both had arrived, in the early days, on the same ships from southern Europe. Succade seems originally to have been a wet sweetmeat, made of citrus fruits or their peels, soaked and boiled several times in plain water to take off their bitterness, and then reboiled in a honey or sugar syrup; and it was sold in its syrup in pots or little barrels. English housewives then learned how to make it themselves, not only from citrus fruits and peels, but also from bitter roots or plant-stalks which had medicinal virtues. They called it 'wet sucket' when the peels or roots remained in their syrup, and 'sucket candy' when they were removed and dried out.

But marmalade was always dry and solid, to be cut with a knife and served in slices. It was imported initially, as we have seen, in a variety of containers, but later often in boxes or small chests. Among the commodities bought on behalf of Lord Robert Dudley in November 1560 for a banquet at Eltham appears 'a brick of marmalade, 2s. 4d. (11 $^{1}/_{2}$ p)'. More marmalade may be concealed within a later entry in the same account, 'for banquetting stuffe bought when the Scottish ambassador dined with your Lordship at Whitehall, 14s. 6d. (72 $^{1}/_{2}$ p).'[15]

Banqueting stuff comprised the sweetmeats and fruits, fresh and preserved, that were offered at the end of a feast or festive meal as a dessert course, intended to ease the laden stomach. In the records of the Skinners' Company of London, an entry taken from the diary of Henry Machin gives an account of the Company's feast of 10 June 1560, and ends '...and Master Clarenshaux made a great banquet for the Masters and the Company, first spiced bread, cherries, strawberries, pippins and marmalade and sucket, comfits and portyngalles (semi-sweet oranges) and divers other dishes, hippocras (spiced wine), Rhenish, claret wine and beer, and all great plenty, and all was welcome.'[16]

The banquet or dessert course was not confined to public or formal entertainments, but became a regular part of the hospitality which the families of the gentry and the people of the middling sort offered to one another. The sweetmeats were provided by the lady of the house who, with her maids, gathered flowers and fruits from her garden during the summer months, and preserved them with the help of sugar for year-round consumption. When a feast or social dinner took place, the company retired at the end of the meal to another room, or in summer to a banqueting house in the garden (landowners constructed summer-houses for the purpose in their grounds). There they drank spiced hippocras and sweet southern wines, and enjoyed a variety of sweetmeats – jellies, sugar pastes, fruits preserved wet in syrup or candied dry with sugar, and the 'tarts of divers hues and sundry denominations, conserves of old fruits, foreign and home-bred suckets, codinacs, marmalades, marchpane (marzipan), sugar-breads, gingerbread, florentines... and sundry outlandish confections altogether seasoned with sugar', listed by William Harrison in his account of the glories of Eliza-bethan England.[17]

The sweetmeats were laid out attractively upon the board, the wet ones in small glasses, the dry ones, including marmalade, piled upon bowls or platters. Painted wooden posy-mats were set before the guests, on which they could lay the items of their choice, so as to enjoy them at their leisure without unduly stickying their fingers.[18] Quince marmalade, imported or, increasingly, home-made, was thus an item for consumption at the end of a meal, eaten for pleasure and as a mild digestive. Sugar retained its earlier reputation of being good for the stomach, so all the sweetmeats were regarded to some extent as aids to digestion. But in the context of the banquet, it is likely that they were no more 'medicinal' than today's finale of a sweet liqueur, or one or two chocolate-coated mints.

MEDICINAL MARMALADE

Quince marmalade, nevertheless, had its niche in popular medical opinion. Quinces were 'cold in the first degree and dry in the beginning of the second', according to Sir Thomas Elyot in *The Castel of Helth,* 1541; but the addition of sugar, which was 'warm', made them a temperate and helpful contribution to the diet. Quinces being 'roasted or sodden (boiled), the core taken out, and mixed with honey clarified or sugar, than they cause good appetite, and preserveth the head from drunkenness', wrote Sir Thomas, and 'taken after meat, it closeth and draweth the stomach together, and helpeth it to digest, and mollifyeth the belly, if it be abundantly taken.'[19] These were the old ideas of Galenic medicine, which had led to the custom of eating first chardequynce, and later marmalade, at the end of a meal, especially a large and heavy one.

Marmalade could be helpful to those in need of a lighter diet, too. Dr LeCoop recommended it to Lady Lisle when he was treating her in the winter of 1538 for an ailment which he diagnosed as having arisen because she was 'of a cold complexion'. He aimed to counterbalance it with a diet including several 'warm' herbs, and the lighter types of fleshmeat, and he limited her to two meals a day, and urged her not to take anything after supper. But if she was constrained to do so, then 'ye shall eat a little marmalade for to comfort your stomach.'[20]

The advantages of marmalade as an aid to digestion were stressed over and over again. John Gerard, noting that quinces were called in Spanish 'codyons, membrillos and marmellos', added that 'the marmalade or cotiniate made of sugar and quinces is good and profitable for the strengthening of the stomach.'[21] William Langham, in *The Garden of Health*, first published in 1579, claimed that marmalade 'is very good to strengthen the stomach, and to keep the meat therein till it be perfectly digested'.[22]

Herein lies the reason for the most famous story about medicinal marmalade, the tradition that it was administered to Mary, Queen of Scots, by her attendants to help her combat sea-sickness on the crossing from Calais to Scotland in 1561. An alternative version suggests that she received the marmalade while she was suffering from a bout of sickness at Jedburgh, where she had a fortified house. She responded with the words, 'Marmalade pour Marie malade', or possibly, 'Marmalade pour ma maladie'– both phrases have come down in different accounts. The tale has led some modern writers to credit Mary with introducing orange marmalade into Britain. But the contemporary medicinal reputation of quince marmalade makes that assumption quite unnecessary. As for Mary's supposed comments, either would be a typical example of the kind of punning that gave such pleasure to the Elizabethans and their Scottish neighbours.

Related to medicinal marmalade, or more accurately to its precursor *cidonitum,* was the confection called *diacitonium.* Its name links it with the Greek medical tradition; many of the remedies of Greek medicine which passed to the medieval West have titles that consist of the word *dia* (through) plus a word denoting the active ingredient. This one, then, achieved its effect through quinces. But on its way west it had picked up the Arab-inspired ingredient of leaf gold, believed to be an elixir of life, or at least an encouragement to health and longevity. The accounts of Sir William Petre of Ingatestone, Essex, record the sum of two shillings (10p) paid for a box of *diacitonium* supplied by his apothecary, when Sir William was suffering from renal stone and general debility.[23]

Diacitonium was made, like quidony, from the strained liquor of boiled quinces reboiled with sugar (a pound to a pound), to which was added four drops of oil of cinnamon and four of oil of nutmegs. But the recipe is printed in *A Closet for Ladies and Gentlewomen,* 1608, under the heading 'Banquetting conceits', so its pretty appearance was already then drawing it away from the medical arena and into that of the decorative dessert sweetmeat. By the time the recipe had reached the seventeenth-century Virginia manuscript book which has survived under the name of *Martha Washington's Booke of Cookery and Booke of Sweetmeats,* the title 'Diacitonium simplex of quinces' had been transmogrified into 'Decocktion of quinces', and its role as a rather flashy sweetmeat was emphasised by the instruction that it was to be stored in 'fine christall glasses'.

MARMALADE AS AN APHRODISIAC

As marmalade became more widely known, so its sweet and delectable nature made it a byword, or image, for such qualities, to be applied in contexts unrelated to either food or medicine. It was an image which appealed to some Elizabethan writers of high-flown prose. Gabriel Harvey and Thomas Walkington both used 'marmalade and sucket' as a figure of speech, to convey the special gifts of the muses.

But marmalade became linked in particular with the sweet aspects of love. 'Thou art as witty a marmalade-eater as ever I conversed with', says Lord Wealthy to Hogge's daughter, whom he is courting, in Robert Tailor's *Hogge hath lost his Pearl,* 1614. Thomas Middleton wrote in 1602 of a Frenchman with 'a soft marmalade heart', and Philip Massinger, in 1629, referred to a kiss withheld in the words 'I cannot blame my lady's unwillingness to part with such marmalade lips.'[24]

Earlier still, two recipes published in *A Closet for Ladies and Gentlewomen,* 1608, indicate that a marmalade could turn out to be a formula for an aphrodisiac. The first is titled, 'To make an excellent marmalade which was given to Queen Mary for a New Yeere's gift'. [See R 7.] As well as sugar and quinces and a flavouring of candied orange-peel well beaten, this marmalade included almonds blanched and beaten, and preserved eringo-roots (sea-holly); and it was flavoured not only with heavily-scented musk and ambergris dissolved in rosewater, but also with cinnamon, ginger, cloves, and mace. Almonds were believed to encourage fertility, and eringo-roots preserved with sugar were a well-known aphrodisiac of Tudor times. Following her marriage to Philip of Spain and until the end of her short reign (1553–8) Mary was desperately anxious to conceive a son, so this excellent marmalade was the offering of a well-wisher to help her achieve her aim. Despite its lack of success, the recipe was preserved, printed, and subsequently recopied into other recipe books; indeed it was put forward with the object of reaching a wider clientele, for the published recipe ends '…and put it into your marmelate boxes, and so present it to whom you please.'

The second recipe follows immediately in *A Closet for Ladies and Gentlewomen,* and bears the title 'To make another sort of Marmelate very comfortable and restorative to any Lord or Lady whatsoever'. [See R 8.] The ingredients show all too clearly what is being restored, for the majority of them are recognised aphrodisiacs of the Elizabethan and Jacobean era: ginger; eringo-roots; cocks' stones or testicles; seeds of red nettles and rocket *(Eruca sativa); scincus marinus* (not a fish, as was sometimes believed, but a small lizard of the Sahara and the Red Sea coast, which was preserved in salt and imported and sold by the apothecaries, because Dioscorides had called it 'a great provocative to lust'); *diasatyrion* (an electuary based upon the orchis, whose roots, also called dogstones, supplied yet another aphrodisiac). Fragments of gold leaf and powdered pearl, also included, were both remedies from Arab medicine, good for the heart and the vital spirits. There are no quinces in this marmalade, though sugar dissolved in rose-water and boiled to a candy is mixed with the other ingredients to help preserve them. Finally the 'marmelate' was gilded, and boxed up, 'and so use it at your pleasure'.

Marmalade did not lose its connection with affairs of the heart, but it gradually went downhill in social terms. John Josselyn described the decorous evening promenade at Boston, a 'rich and very populous' town when he visited it on his second voyage to New England in 1663. 'On the South there is a small but pleasant Common where the gallants a little before sunset walk with their Marmelet-madams, as we do in Moorfields, &c. till the nine o'clock bell rings them home to their respective habitations, when presently the Constables walk their rounds to see good order kept.'[25] The status of the marmalade-madams had declined by 1727 when 'More marmulet madams will be met strolling in the fields than honest women in the streets', according to Edward Ward.[26] They had become the women of easy virtue, out taking the air.

The marmalade-madams are at the tail-end of a tradition that stemmed from the welcome given to sweet, comforting quince marmalade in Tudor times. Marmalade itself had moved on to new manifestations, and these must now be examined.

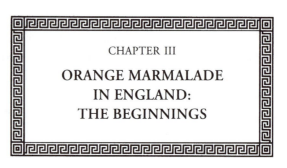

CHAPTER III

ORANGE MARMALADE
IN ENGLAND:
THE BEGINNINGS

MARMALADES OF OTHER FRUITS

Quince marmalade was the basic form of the conserve, the one that the Tudor and Stuart preserving books simply designated as 'marmalade', often without further qualification. Marmalades of other fruits always had to have their fruits named. Such marmalades had not been slow to appear. *The Secrets of Alexis of Piedmont,* translated into English in 1562, concluded its instructions for the making of quince marmalade by saying, 'In like manner may you dress and trim peaches, pears, and other kinds of fruits.'

The method by which fruits were boiled soft and then reboiled with sugar was obviously applicable to any fruits, hard or otherwise; and so a series of recipes for non-quince marmalades made their appearance. John Partridge's *The Treasurie of Commodious Conceites and Hidden Secrets,* 1584, has one titled, 'To make marmalade of damsons or prunes', with the plums boiled soft and strained through a coarse boulter 'as ye make a tart (i.e. a tart-filling)', before being reboiled with sugar. 'This wise you may make marmalade of wardens, pears, apples and medlars, services (fruit of the service-tree, related to the rowan), checkers or strawberries, every one by himself, or mix it together, as you think good.' The 1587 edition of *A Book of Cookrye* by A.W. contained a 'dry marmalade of peaches'. [See R 5.] Peaches and pears and several other fruits are poorer in pectin than quinces. Furthermore, there was a strong tendency in Tudor times to overcook all foods in terms of today's standards. So many of the so-called marmalades must have turned out as fruit-and-sugar pastes, in which the sugar recrystallised almost as soon as they were cold.

Recipes for the marmalades of home-grown fruits other than quinces appeared in the preserving books all through the seventeenth century. The later ones show a somewhat softer conserve, still dense and sticky, but potted, not boxed, made from such fruits as raspberries, mulberries, cherries, white or red currants, gooseberries, apricots or damsons, and it was for this type of conserve that the name 'jam' was coined.

Apples, however, proved to have jelling qualities comparable with those of quinces themselves, provided they were the right kind of apples, not too sweet and not too ripe – 'the quickest pippins when they are newly-gathered and are sharp', as Sir Kenelm Digby put it.[1] Pippins were semi-sweet apples, originally raised from pips, and a number of varieties had been bred by the seventeenth century. Marmalade of pippins was a preserve made quite regularly then, to judge by its frequent appearances in recipe books. Sometimes it was made from the pulp of the pippins, and sometimes it was a jelly, produced from the juice strained from pippins boiled in a little water. It was to provide a link in the chain leading to the development of orange marmalade.

THE FIRST ORANGE MARMALADE

The Arabs brought orange- and lemon-trees to southern Europe, along with the methods of irrigation which allowed them to flourish through rainless summers in Spain and Portugal, Sicily and southern Italy; and afterwards to bear fruit. The oranges were bitter, of the type of the Seville orange. Sweet orange-trees grew even then, near the coasts of Palestine at the eastern end of the Mediterranean, but they bore inferior and tasteless oranges, and were little valued. Eventually, in the early sixteenth century, the Portuguese were to bring back from further east a flavourful semi-sweet orange (known in English as a Portingall), and a hundred years later the true, sweet, China orange. But the orange of the Middle Ages was bitter, its sour juice welcomed as a relish and in sauces. The peel was not wasted. The Arabs had also introduced sugar-cane in the orange-growing regions of the West. With sugar, orange- and lemon-peels could be conserved either dry or in syrup, to be kept for culinary or medicinal use, with their bitterness and sharpness mitigated, while their tangy flavour was retained in a more delicious form.

Both sugar and the succade made with citrus peels or whole fruits were exported to the northern European countries. The bitter oranges themselves, along with lemons, also arrived there, rare and costly at first. But by the end of the Middle Ages they were becoming more plentiful, and were sold at prices within reach of both the well-to-do and the folk of the middling sort. The orange-juice supplied sour sauces, and the peels were also welcomed, since they could be turned into home-made succade, both delectable and health-promoting.

As the technique of making marmalade from quinces or any other fruits became better known during the sixteenth century, it was applied to oranges too; and some of the earliest English recipes show signs of a southern origin. Thus the recipe for 'Conserve of oranges' in A.W.'s *Book of Cookrye*, 1587, offers a method of making it by soaking and boiling oranges in water to remove their bitterness, and then beating them small with a spoon. Then, 'put to every pound of oranges one pound of sugar and half a pound of rosewater, and boil them together and box them.' The peel of Seville oranges is rich in pectin, so this confection would have had something of the jellied quality associated with quince marmalade, and it may have been even more solid.

Sir Hugh Plat, in *Delightes for Ladies,* 1605, explained how 'To preserve oranges after the Portugall fashion'. Here 24 whole oranges are prepared and put into a sugar syrup, in the manner of wet sucket.[2] Next, 8 of them are beaten and mixed with sugar to a paste which is divided up and stuffed into the central cavity of each of the other 16; '...and so boil them again in your syrup; then there will be marmalade of oranges within your oranges, and it will cut like a hard egg.' [See R10.]

Gervase Markham's 'Excellent marmalade of oranges', published in the 1631 edition of *The English Huswife,* was very close to A.W.'s 'Conserve of oranges'. Other seventeenth-century recipes of comparable type required only the peels of the soaked and prepared oranges to be pounded up, and made up the rest of the bulk with boiled and beaten pippins, presumably in the hope of securing a firmer set. Others again boiled the citrus fruits whole, added whole boiled pippins, and pressed them together through a sieve or strainer before reboiling with sugar. [See R 11.] All the orange marmalades made by these methods were of solid consistency, and were boxed for keeping in the manner of quince marmalade. They were to be the progenitors of one of the two principal types of English orange marmalade of the eighteenth and early nineteenth centuries.

MARMALADE OF PIPPINS AND JELLY OF PIPPINS

For the origin of the other type we have to examine the seventeenth-century marmalades of pippins, and especially those for which only the jelly from the pippin liquid was used. Apple jelly has a delicate flavour, too delicate for an age which loved spices and strong-tasting foods. The marmalade of pippins in *A Daily Exercise for Ladies and Gentlewomen,* 1617, was therefore confected with rosewater, cinnamon water and beaten fennel seeds. But other recipes show that some people flavoured their pippin jelly with a little grated lemon- and orange-peel, and added lemon juice to sharpen the taste (and, although they may not have realised it, to improve the set).

The 1650s saw a further advance. *A True Gentlewoman's Delight* was published in 1653.[3] Here there are instructions for making a 'jelly of pippins' for which the pippins are boiled, strained gently through canvas, and the liquor reboiled with sugar, with lemon-juice added when it is almost ready to jell. Then comes the further addition of orange-peel, which had previously been soaked and boiled soft, and is now cut into 'long pieces, then put it into the syrup and stir it about, and fill your glasses, and let it stand till it be cold, and then it is ready to eat.' Jellies of pippins with shredded orange-peel in them were still dishes for the banquet or dessert, but took their place along with the sweet jellies rather than with the dry sweetmeats.

'Sr. Kenelme Digby, Kt.' Sir K. Digby, *Choice and Experimental Receipts in Physick and Chirurgery*, 2nd ed. 1675.

Two years later appeared the first edition of *The Queen's Closet Opened*, 'transcribed from the true copies of Her Majesties [Queen Henrietta Maria] by W.M., one of her servants'; and in that book was a very similar recipe in which 'long threads of orange peels' and also finely-cut slices of lemon were boiled in the sweetened pippin liquor, and then laid in a glass container into which the jelly-liquor was poured. The glass displayed to advantage the clarity of the jelly and the shreds of orange peel and lemon slices suspended in it.

Finally, the elaborate preserved pippins of Sir Kenelm Digby's friend Lady Paget deserve a mention. The apples 'finely pared and whole' were boiled with sugar in the liquor strained from other pippins until it was about to jell. Then they were lapped in complete orange-skins which had been skilfully removed in one piece, and softened and preserved in syrup in the usual way. Sir Kenelm's comment on this recipe was: 'I conceive Apple Johns instead of pippins will do better, both for the jelly and the syrup, especially at the latter end of the year; and I like them thin-sliced rather than whole; and the orange-peels scattered among them in little pieces or chips.'

All these recipes and the others like them raise questions about the time of year when the conserves were made. The early autumn, when the apples were newly-picked and their pectin content was at its highest, was too soon for the oranges to be ripe. The pippins could be stored, of course, and the lemon-juice, which is often an ingredient, would have supplemented their reduced pectin. Another solution, to be found in several recipes, was to use sliced candied orange peel, prepared during the previous orange season. [See R 12.]

The idea of cutting orange-peel into the shreds or chips which were later to characterise British marmalade can be traced back to this period, and in particular to the pippin jellies and marmalades invented by members of the circle of the Court of King Charles II. It was a circle with a deep interest in food and in trying out unusual dishes, an interest fostered by the sojourn in France during the king's exile and continued after his restoration to England. Several of those concerned also travelled elsewhere in Europe, and learned from the new food experiences offered by countries other than France.

French influence of an indirect kind may have caused the type of recipe which had formerly been called pippin jelly to have its name changed, first to marmalade of pippins, and then to marmalade of oranges. Hitherto English marmalade had always been a solid, thick, dry conserve of quinces or of other fruits brought to a similar consistency after being boiled with sugar. In France the equivalent thick quince conserve was called *cotignac espais*. But La Varenne showed that a thinner version with a softer jelly could be made by boiling the quinces and sugar together for a shorter time, and gave the French name for this thinner jellied quince conserve as 'marmalade de coings'.[4] It was put up in faience pots. It may have been the consistency of the thinner French 'marmelade' which encouraged some English noble ladies – and gentlemen – to call an English pippin jelly, which was likewise of a consistency to be stored in pots or glasses, by the name of marmalade.

TRUE ORANGE MARMALADE

A truly orange marmalade now emerged, made from Seville oranges set by their pectin without any assistance from pippins, and this too was potted, not boxed. The inventor is unknown; or perhaps different versions of this type of conserve were invented separately in a number of gentry households. Too many of the hand-written cookery and preserving books of the seventeenth century have been lost for us to know. But one very early maker of true orange marmalade was the mother of Rebecca Price. Rebecca copied the instructions for 'marmelett of oringes: my mother's receipt' into her own recipe book in 1681.[5] This marmalade begins with the rind of the best Seville oranges sliced very thin and boiled in two waters until tender. Then the peels, the pulp and a pound of sugar for every four oranges were heated very slowly together. 'So keepe it with continual stirring till you think it be enough ...it will not be stiff as other marmelett, to be cutt, but must be taken out with spoons.' Nevertheless, it would certainly have been equivalent to the thickest orange marmalades made today, and perhaps thicker still.

The printed cookery-books did not at once reflect the new trend. These publications tended to lag somewhat when new fashions emerged, since so many of their recipes were copied out of earlier books. In *The Whole Duty of a Woman*, 1737, is an orange marmalade recipe which not only includes apple pulp, but also still adds half a pint of rosewater.

But while the later seventeenth-century printed books remained faithful to pippins as an ingredient of orange marmalade, they do at least show that the idea of a softer, potted preserve was making headway. 'When it is enough, put it into flat pots or glasses, and when it is cold, paper it up and set it in your closet', says *The True Way of Preserving and Candying* in 1681. But the recipe then continues, 'You may make cakes of the same to dry', and gives instructions for spreading out the cooked paste on plates and exposing it to warm air in a stove.

Even though versions of the potted preserve became more and more common in recipe-books, the old, solid, boxed marmalade lingered on for some time. In the earliest Scottish printed cookery-book of 1737, Mrs McLintock had recipes for a 'marmalet of gooseberries' to be put up in 'marmalet-boxes', and one of apples 'in marmalet-boxes, or thin galleypots'. Her orange marmalade, however, was to be poured into pots. Hannah Glasse, ten years later, ended her potted marmalade recipe in *The Art of Cookery* by saying, 'If you would have it cut like marmalade, add some jelly of pippins, and allow sugar for it.' The sentence was repeated in every later edition until 1778, when solid marmalade must have been abandoned by even the most conservative of families, for in the 1784 edition it had finally disappeared.

A recipe for pippin-free orange marmalade was printed at last in Mary Kettilby's *A Collection of above Three Hundred Receipts,* garnered from 'a number of very curious and delicate housewives' in 1714. It was for a beaten or pounded marmalade. To make it, the juice was squeezed from the oranges, and their pulp and peel were boiled and then pounded together; then sugar, the orange-juice and a generous allowance of lemon-juice were added, and a final reboiling took place. [See R 14.] Other pippin-free orange marmalade recipes followed in the published recipe-books, some with and some without the lemon-juice, which would have been a useful source both of acid and of pectin. While beaten orange marmalades remained popular, most cookery-books of the eighteenth century gave alternative instructions for marmalades in which the orange-peel was added in the form of finely-cut shreds or chips. Both styles of marmalade coexisted for a great many years.

Although marmalade itself had now changed in character from the sliced conserve eaten at the Elizabethan and Jacobean banquet course, marmalade usage was not greatly different. In England marmalade was served in its jellied, potted form as an item for the dessert, which had succeeded the earlier banquet. The dessert sometimes formed a separate course, but during the eighteenth century was often laid out as part of the second course, with candied fruits, fruit jellies, glasses of marmalade, syllabubs, fruit creams, and other such delights, placed on a dessert frame in the centre of the table.

MEDICINAL ORANGE MARMALADE

Orange marmalade took its place at the end of a meal because quince marmalade and succade were served at that stage. Quince marmalade, like its predecessor chardequynce, helped to close the stomach and aided digestion, according to medical opinion. The

To make Orange-Marmalade, *very good.*

TAKE eighteen fair large *Sevil-*Oranges, pare them very thin, then cut them in halves, and fave their Juice in a clean Veffel, and fet it cover'd in a cool Place; put the half-Oranges into Water for one Night, then boil them very tender, fhifting the Water 'till all the Bitternefs is out, then dry them well, and pick out the Seeds and Strings as nicely as you can; pound them fine, and to every pound of Pulp take a pound of double-refin'd Sugar; boil your Pulp and Sugar almoft to a Candy-height: When this is ready, you muft take the Juice of fix Lemons, the Juice of all the Oranges, ftrain it, and take its full weight in double-refin'd Sugar, all which pour in to the Pulp and Sugar; and boil the whole pretty faft 'till it will Jelly. Keep your Glaffes cover'd, and 'twill be a lafting wholfome Sweet-meat for any Ufe.

Orange marmalade, 1714. M. Kettilby, *A Collection of above Three Hundred Receipts in Cookery, Physic and Surgery*, 1714.

medical reasons for serving succade (the preparation of orange- or lemon-peels in syrup) at that stage were not quite so obvious. The physician Andrew Boorde wrote in 1542, 'Oranges doth make a man to have a good appetite, and so do the rinds, if they be in succade.'[6] It appears that candied orange-peel, when eaten medicinally, was sometimes taken at the beginning of a meal, rather than the end. The rind of Seville oranges was 'hot in the first degree and dry in the second', according to Sir Thomas Elyot; and he also said, 'The rinds taken in a little quantity, do comfort the stomach, where it digesteth, specially condite [candied] with sugar, and taken fasting in a small quantity.'[7] This represented popular dietary lore which was to lead eventually, in Scotland, to marmalade being taken, fasting, at the beginning of the day, at the meal which broke the nightly fast.[8]

In the meantime, orange marmalade carried a good reputation, not only as a stomachic, but also as a cure for rheums, coughs and colds. It was on a list of medicaments which his apothecary supplied to Sir William Jopson when he was suffering from a violent cough and pains in his side in December 1665. On the apothecary's account are many varied remedies, including night-pills gilded with wafer-gold, brown candy (our 'cough-candy'), a box of sugar of roses, and, for the 25th of the month, a glass of lavender water (possessing, according to Culpeper, a 'hot and subtle spirit'; it was formerly taken internally), a bought quilted night-cap and 'a glass of orenge Marmalade'.[9]

Orange-peel 'condite with sugar' was regarded also as a cordial, that is, as something which revives and strengthens the heart. The quality was recognised in the case of candied orange-peel chips, another seventeenth-century favourite. The recipe, 'To candy orange-peels after the Italian way' in *The Queen's Closet Opened*, 1655, adds: '*The virtues:* They corroborate the heart and stomach.' Orange marmalade, likewise, was seen as having cordial, as well as cold-curing and stomachic properties. The first two were urged by William Salmon on behalf of his recipe for a marmalade of oranges, lemons and pippins in *The Family Dictionary*, second edition, 1696, for he explained, 'This is a very good cordial and stoppeth the rheum.'

The appetite-provoking properties of citrus-fruit marmalade continued to be recognised all through the nineteenth century and into the twentieth. Its cordial aspects gradually dwindled away. Nor is it often taken as a cold-cure nowadays. Yet there may have been some grounds for believing it could cure cold diseases. Not all the vitamin C in the peel and juice of Seville oranges is lost, even after the prolonged boiling which they undergo in marmalade-making. During the seventeenth century, fresh fruit and vegetables were still viewed with suspicion by medical men (although the antiscorbutic effects of preparations of scurvygrass and other herbs had by then been discovered, and these were taken in the spring as an antidote to the mild scurvy brought on by the winter diet). The vitamin C in orange marmalade, little though it was, may have been enough to help some people of those days to throw off their colds and coughs.

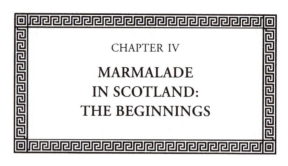

CHAPTER IV

MARMALADE
IN SCOTLAND:
THE BEGINNINGS

As the history of marmalade unfolded in Britain, it was in England that the earliest initiatives were taken, in importing quince marmalade and in the home production of both quince and orange marmalades. During the eighteenth century that situation was to change, for not only were the Scots then making their own orange marmalade according to recipes which paralleled those of England, but they were also in the lead in introducing a new pattern for marmalade consumption.

Marmalade's role in Scotland before that time is rather obscure. Mary, Queen of Scots, may have 'introduced' quince marmalade to fellow Scots, but it was a foreign import which initially must have come with her on the ship from Calais. It was perhaps only the irresistible temptation of the famous pun on her name which prevented its arriving under its French designation of *cotignac*.[1] Thereafter more quince marmalade was doubtless imported into Scotland from time to time, as a luxury to be consumed at the

Scottish court and among the gentry, but little of it can ever have been made there.

Unlike the English gentlewomen of the southern counties, few Scottish gentlewomen could produce marmalade from their own garden quinces. The east coast and the hinterland were far too cold to allow quince trees to bear fruit. Perhaps quinces were raised successfully in a few great gardens near the west coast, especially in the eighteenth century, when gardeners had learned to protect tender fruit trees with heated walls and similar devices. There are no records to tell us.[2] Lady Castlehill, who owned a fertile estate on the banks of the Clyde, certainly had a quince marmalade recipe in her household book of 1712; but were the five quinces it required grown in her garden, or brought to her by visitors from further south; or was the recipe simply copied from a southern friend? Whatever the answer, it is significant that the eighteenth-century cookery-books printed and published in Scotland either omit quince marmalade, or include a single token recipe, in contrast to the two or three quince marmalade recipes in most English cookery-books of the period.

Early Scottish household books do contain some other marmalades, however, for Lady Castlehill has marmalade of gooseberries and marmalade of wardens (pears), and Mrs McClintock published recipes for marmalade of apples and marmalade of gooseberries in 1736. These marmalades, at least, could have been made without difficulty from locally-grown fruits.

Oranges were a different matter. They had been coming in by sea since the end of the fifteenth century. Their first mention occurs in the accounts of the Lord Treasurer which show a payment of 3 shillings on 24 April 1497 'for bearing the apple-oranges to the house [in Leith] from the ship'; and one of 12 pence 'for one small barrel to send apple-oranges to Falkland and Saint Andrews to the King'. The Spanish ambassador was in Scotland in 1497 to negotiate a peace between King James IV of Scotland and King Henry

VII of England, and the oranges may have arrived on the same ship.[3] 'Apple-oranges' translates the medieval Latin terms for oranges, *mala arancia* and *pomarancia*.

Further shipments of oranges and lemons reached Leith, Edinburgh and Glasgow from time to time, though they would hardly have arrived there in such large numbers as they did at Bristol or London. But by the end of the seventeenth century they were being purchased not infrequently for gentry households (oranges cost 2d. (under 1p) and lemons 5d. (over 2p) each, and orange-peel, from the confectioners, 1s. 11d. (nearly 10p) a pound).[4] The cuisine of the Scottish gentry grew closer to that of their English counterparts after the Union of 1603. Lady Castlehill's recipes were transcribed in 1712, but most of them are rather old-fashioned, and they show close affinities with English seventeenth-century dishes. Oranges, or their juice, were used from time to time as a flavouring or garnish; and the fruits were also candied, were preserved whole in pippin jelly, or were made into marmalade. This last recipe shows a typical seventeenth-century beaten marmalade, which includes some pippin-pulp along with the boiled and pounded skins and pulp of the oranges.

A new stimulus was given to marmalade-making, and also to the candying of oranges and other fruits in Scotland when the sugar-boiling houses were established, three in Glasgow and one in Leith, between 1667 and 1701.[5] Citrus fruits may have arrived along with the raw sugar shipped from southern Europe, and occasionally even on the vessels carrying West Indian sugar, for there is evidence that oranges were sent from the Indies to Europe in those pre-steamship days, despite the long voyage.[6] Lady Castlehill wrote that pickled lemons could be bought from the confectioners. The confectioners also sold sugar-preserved fruits, candied orange-chips and the like, and it is probable that in Edinburgh and Glasgow they purveyed ready-made orange marmalade for those who did not wish to make their own.

Orange tree. J. Gerard, *The Herball*, 1597.

The first English printed recipe for orange marmalade, unassisted by pippins or pippin-juice, was probably that published by Mary Kettilby in 1714, and it was for beaten marmalade, with the orange-peel and pulp boiled soft and pounded in a mortar. The earliest Scottish printed recipe, 'To make marmalet of oranges and lemons', in Mrs McLintock's *Receipts* of 1736, is also for beaten marmalade (the lemons do not appear anywhere in it, so probably the original recipe, like several others, once terminated with words to the effect that 'Thus also may you make marmalade of lemons'; but the sentence was dropped owing to the rarity of lemon marmalade in Scotland). [See R 15.]

In England, the shredded-peel orange marmalades were also made throughout the eighteenth century and their popularity was reflected by their frequent appearances in the cookery-books. Eliza Smith in 1727 had one for which the Seville orange skins were to be cut 'as thin as palates' (a fricasee of ox-palates is a delicacy described elsewhere in her book) and boiled clear and tender before being reboiled into marmalade with the orange-pulp and lemon-juice. Her second orange marmalade, which included pippin jelly, also had the rinds cut 'very fine'. Hannah Glasse's version of orange marmalade (1747) was made with 'peel that is shred'; and Elizabeth Raffald (1769), who had one recipe for beaten orange marmalade, had another for transparent marmalade, with the peels cut in very fine slices and the marmalade boiled until both peels and jelly were clear and transparent. [See R17.]

The Scottish cookery-books soon followed suit. Elizabeth Cleland in the 1700s had both beaten and shredded-peel marmalades made from a single composite recipe, with the oranges given a preliminary boiling and then divided into two groups for separate treatment; and she called the slivers of shredded peel for her second kind of marmalade 'chips'.

Susanna MacIver, whose *Cookery and Pastry* was first published in 1773, gave separate recipes for both types under the titles 'smooth marmalade' and 'chip marmalade'.

These early Scottish recipes naming the shredded orange-peels as 'chips' show how this word was already becoming the favourite Scottish term for the finely-cut peels of marmalade-making. It may have originated with candied orange-peel chips, a separate item of confectionery prepared on both sides of the border and well liked even before the days of shredded-peel marmalades. In England marmalade with finely-cut peel, set by its own pectin, was known for a long time as transparent marmalade, following Elizabeth Raffald's use of this name for her recipe of 1769. In Scotland it was called chip marmalade. Its fame spread to such an extent that Richard Abbott, in *The Housekeeper's Valuable Present* published in London about 1800, put in a special instruction under the heading 'Scotch marmalade': 'When you make your orange marmalade [his recipe is for beaten marmalade], put a little by; then cut some orange-peel into fine strips, and giving them a boil in a little clarified sugar, mix them in the marmalade, and put them into pots.'

MARMALADE AT THE SCOTTISH BREAKFAST TABLE: THE EIGHTEENTH CENTURY

The most striking contribution of the Scots to the history of marmalade is not, however, to be sought in the realm of recipes. It lay in the transferring of the conserve to a new mealtime position, as part of the first meal of the day. The medicinal virtues of orange-peel 'condite with sugar, and taken fasting in a small quantity', as recommended by Sir Thomas Elyot, had not been forgotten.[7] Both the peel and the sugar were warming to the cold early morning stomach.

The Scots had their own way of warming the stomach at the beginning of the day, by drinking a dram of whisky, and following it up with ale with a toast swimming in it. This pattern of break-fasting was disturbed when tea-drinking began to grow popular in Scotland, early in the eighteenth century. Some people continued with the customary dram, but replaced the ale with tea. Others replaced the dram as well, and ate warming sugar-preserved orange-peel or orange marmalade in its stead.

It was William Macintosh of Borlum who first published a com-plaint about the new practice in 1729. 'When I came to my friend's house in a morning, I used to be asked if I had my morning draught yet? I am now asked, if I have yet had my tea? And in lieu of the big quaigh [drinking-cup, originally of staved wood] with strong ale and toast, and after a dram of good wholesome Scots spirits, there is now the tea-kettle put to the fire, the tea-table, and silver and China equipage brought in, with the marmalet, cream and cold tea.'[8] The rest of the passage makes it quite plain that the writer disapproved of the innovation.

Others were more complimentary. Later in the century Scottish breakfasts became famed for their excellence among English tra-vellers. Oatcakes and toasted bread, butter, honey and preserves made from local berries were added to the marmalade; and some-times there were cold meats and potted meats, or newly-caught fish as well. The dram of whisky was often retained, too. Samuel Johnson partook of it during his journey to the western islands of Scotland in 1773. He gave an enthusiastic report on the Scottish breakfast:

> Not long after the dram, may be expected the breakfast, a meal in which the Scots, whether of the lowlands or moun-tains, must be confessed to excel us. The tea and coffee are accompanied, not only with butter, but with honey, con-serves, and marmalades.[9]

During the same Scottish tour, James Boswell, on the Isle of Raasay, wrote of 'coffee and tea in genteel order upon the table, as it was past six when we arrived: diet loaf [very light spiced sponge cake], marmalade of oranges, currant jelly.'

He was again offered the marmalade and jelly for breakfast next morning, with 'as good chocolate as I ever tasted, tea, and bread and butter.'[10] He bore witness to the popularity of marmalade in Scotland, eaten both at an evening tea-drinking and at breakfast. More than fifty years later Margaret Dods referred to orange marmalade 'used at breakfast or tea', in *The Cook and Housewife's Manual.*

Many Scottish marmalades, like English marmalades of the period, continued very dense and sticky, though no longer solid and dry enough to slice. They may have been somewhat difficult to deal with, even with the help of a spoon. Eventually, as an afterthought in the third edition of *The Cook and Housewife's Manual*, 1828, Margaret Dods offered advice on the matter: 'Orange-marmalade ... may be thinned with apple jelly, or when used at breakfast or tea, it may be liquefied *ex tempore* with a little tea.'

JANET KEILLER'S INITIATIVE

It has long been a tradition that Janet Keiller, wife of a Dundee grocer, was the inventor of orange marmalade. F. Marian McNeill tried to identify Janet more closely and found two Janet Keillers, an earlier one, née Pierson, who was married to James Keiller in 1700 (the record of her marriage is in the Dundee register); and a later Janet, nee Matthewson and wife of John Keiller, a descendant of the original James, who with her son, also James, established the firm of James Keiller and Son in 1797.[11] The story runs as follows:

The husband of one of the Janets (Miss McNeill believed it was the first, but the Keiller Company's own account suggests it was the second) bought a load of Seville oranges cheaply from a storm-driven ship which had taken shelter in Dundee harbour, at an unknown date in the eighteenth century. Janet was able to turn the oranges into marmalade with the help of her husband's stock of sugar; and it sold so successfully in his shop that in due course the firm of James Keiller and Son was established to manufacture and sell such marmalade as a full-scale commercial enterprise. The firm was founded in 1797, presumably not too long after Janet's original marmalade sales had demonstrated that the market was ready for her conserve (which again points to the second Janet, the mother of James, as the maker).

It is most unlikely that she needed to invent a recipe to cope with her abundance of oranges, for so many were in circulation at that period. She, and her friends, would surely have had their own family marmalade recipes. Even if that had not been the case, then somewhere in Dundee there must have been available one or two copies of the recipe books of McLintock, or Cleland, or MacIver, or Frazer, or of such English counterparts as E. Smith, Glasse or Raffald; and any of these could have supplied viable recipes. The presence of the oranges themselves is sufficient guarantee of the popularity of Seville orange marmalade in Scotland at the time. The lost and storm-tossed ship was not apparently heading for Dundee in the first place; but it could have been bound for Leith, its stock of oranges intended for the markets of Leith and Edinburgh for the use of marmalade-makers there.

Janet Keiller did not invent orange marmalade. But she contributed to the establishment of the 'chip' version as Scotland's very own marmalade. The eighteenth-century Scottish cookery-books carried recipes for both beaten, alias 'smooth', marmalade and for chip marmalade. Janet, faced with vast numbers of oranges, had to make a decision about which type to prepare, and she perhaps found it marginally less laborious to shred or 'chip' the peels than to pound them to a pulp in a mortar. For chip marmalade was the type for which James Keiller and Son became known and there is no reason to doubt that the company's choice in this matter followed Janet's initiative.

Again, Janet and her husband John were not the first people to offer marmalade for sale, for pots of marmalade were almost certainly on the shelves of eighteenth-century confectioners' shops in Scotland, as well as in England. But it was perhaps the size of Janet's operation which made her son James realise that a large-scale market for manufactured marmalade could be found, not only in Dundee but very soon also in Edinburgh and before long in distant London and other English cities.

The firm of James Keiller expanded quickly after 1797. It is recorded that James's younger brother invented a machine for cutting the orange-peel into strips, and marmalade production was moved to a specially-built manufactory in the heart of Dundee. Dundee marmalade became a byword in Scotland and frequently formed part of the Scottish breakfast which still held its own as an example of excellence. Walter Scott recalled breakfasts at the house of his friend Dalgleish, at his estate on the Clyde: 'Such breakfasts we used to have at Kilmardinnie: fresh trout, game pies, cold venison, a baron of beef on the sideboard, home-made scones, potato scones, white puddings, and Scotch baps, to say nothing of Dundee marmalade and Scotch bannocks.'[12]

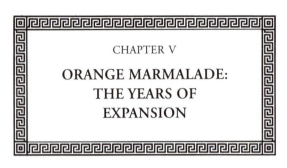

CHAPTER V

ORANGE MARMALADE:
THE YEARS OF
EXPANSION

ENGLISH MARMALADE: DESSERT SWEETMEAT INTO BREAKFAST FARE

The two principal varieties of orange marmalade, the beaten or 'smooth' and the jellied with shredded peel, both continued in vogue in England through the 1700s and into the 1800s. The latter type, which became known as transparent marmalade, had the visual advantage. Elizabeth Raffald gave careful instructions that the final boiling of the ingredients should last for twenty minutes, 'and if it is not clear and transparent, boil it five or six minutes longer, keep stirring it gently all the time, and take care you do not break the slices; when it is cold, put it into jelly or sweetmeat glasses, tie them down with brandy papers over them. They are pretty for a dessert of any kind.' [See R 17.]

The custom of serving marmalade as a dessert dish persisted still longer. Mrs Rundell added to her recipes for beaten orange marmalade and beaten lemon marmalade in the 1807 (corrected) edition of her *A New System of Domestic Cookery* the advice that 'they are very good and elegant sweetmeats'. Their recipes were placed alongside those for other sweet dessert dishes; and the general instruction given at the end of the book was that they were suitable to be set out at the second course of a dinner. In 1807 this was still true.

Mrs Rundell's book was reissued in edition after edition almost yearly until the late 1830s, with her comments on marmalade and on the appropriate foods for the two courses unchanged. But by then other changes had taken place. The old arrangement whereby all dishes were placed on the table to form only two large courses was replaced at great dinners by the service *à la russe* (several courses, with individual items brought to the diners by servants), and at lesser ones by four or more separate courses. The dessert still followed the final course, but it became simpler, comprising bowls or plates of fresh fruits, preserved whole or sliced fruits, dried fruits and nuts, and ices. And marmalade ceased to be a dessert sweet-meat.

But it had already begun to move into its new role in England as well as in Scotland. In *The Times* of 24 March 1815 the following advertisement appeared:

> Orange Marmalade – the admirers of that admirable and nutritious substitute for butter are respectfully informed that they may be supplied with a very superior article at 2s. 6d. [12 $^1/_2$ p] a pound by R. Sewell, pastry-cook and confectioner, 6 Tichborne Street, Golden Square and 239 Piccadilly, 5 doors from the Haymarket; letters post paid.[1]

Marmalade was on sale in London, and in this case was being specially made for a high-class confectioner. Significant in the advertisement is the comparison between marmalade and butter, for it indicates that the new trend towards treating marmalade as a 'spread' was already under way. Margaret Dods, in the 1800s, wrote of Scottish marmalade 'prepared in large quantities for exportation', no doubt by several different small firms, though none were to prove to be survivors, as Keiller was; and she said that the prepared and cut-up oranges were 'put at once into a thin syrup and boiled for from four to six hours, and potted in large jars.' Such prolonged boiling would have weakened the pectin set, even though it may have driven off much of the additional moisture in the sugar-syrup; so the exported marmalades may well have been thinner than eighteenth-century orange marmalades and thus more amenable to spreading.

Again, John Galt's gentle mockery of Jenny MacBride and Mrs Pringle in *The Ayrshire Legatees*, 1821, suggests that marmalade was quite easily obtainable in London at that time. Miss MacBride had given her friend a pot of 'marmalet' at Glasgow, 'assuring me that it was not only dainteous, but a curiosity among the English.' Mrs Pringle was bound for London by sea, but she broke the marmalade pot in nailing down her box of assorted possessions before the voyage began, and thereafter it did great damage to her muslin gown packed in paper, while the syrup from the marmalade even managed to mix itself with the brine from her butter and then to spoil her cheese, as the sea rocked the contents of her box.

Galt was in the habit of showing Scottish visitors around London, and the stories he garnered from some of the more naive among them provided material for his novel. The point of the present tale seems to be that marmalade was very far from being a curiosity in contemporary London, and that the accident and its sad consequences therefore need never have happened.[2]

Marmalade continued as a popular conserve in England, with its usage as a breakfast spread taking over from its former role as dessert dish on the pattern already established for the Scottish breakfast. Its appearance at the English dinner-table became confined to the marmalade tartlets sometimes served at formal dinners in the sweet course preceding the dessert, and to the homelier marmalade puddings of the everyday family dinner.

ORANGE MARMALADE RECIPES: SOME NEW DEVELOPMENTS

Beaten orange marmalade, which eventually became known in some circles as English marmalade, in contrast to Scottish chip marmalade, went out of fashion during the middle decades of the nineteenth century. For a breakfast spread the chip marmalade was perhaps the first choice, but when a jelly conserve was preferred then a clear, transparent marmalade with a little finely-cut peel or no peel at all became the usual kind. Beaten marmalade was the oldest form of orange marmalade, a direct descendant of the type of marmalade which in Sir Hugh Plat's recipe of 1605 had supplied the filling for preserved oranges 'after the Portugall fashion'. [See R 10 and R 14.] It is now another of the lost foodstuffs of Britain.

Most eighteenth-century marmalades, whether of the beaten or chip variety, had been of a thick consistency, for little liquid went into their composition other than that supplied by the juice of the oranges. As a result, their flavour was so highly concentrated that some people found it too strong, despite the fact that the oranges were usually presoaked and boiled several times 'to take out the bitterness'. Quite early in the eighteenth century the custom arose of rasping or grating the orange-peels at the beginning of marmalade-making to mollify the flavour. This had to be done with care, for if too much of the outer skin with its aromatic oils was lost the marmalade became insipid. Susanna MacIver recognised that the operation could be a way of controlling the degree of bitterness of the conserve, since part of what was removed was often mixed in again later on. 'You may keep out some of the grate,' she wrote, 'unless you chuse it very bitter. If you save any of the grate, dry and keep it for seasonings.'

Margaret Dods in 1826 said that, in the making of 'Scotch orange-chip marmalade … if the chips look too numerous, part of them may be withheld for pudding-seasoning. The orange-grate, if a strong flavour is wanted, may either be added in substance, or infused, and the tincture strained and added to the marmalade when boiling.'

These devices helped reduce the overstrong flavour of the con-centrated marmalades of the day, but the final solution was to lie in the addition of more water. A little water already entered into some early orange marmalades because it was used with frothed egg-whites to clarify the sugar, which was then added as a hot syrup. Vigorous boiling of the marmalade was often recommended to try to drive out the extra moisture; and the finished product must have suffered from crystallisation of the sugar if it was stored for any length of time.

In the later eighteenth century, there was a move to increase the amount of water in marmalade recipes. Charlotte Mason, in 1775, suggested half a pint of water to a pound of sugar and a pound of orange-pulp, and these proportions were repeated in recipes over the next hundred years, even appearing in the first (1861) edition of Mrs Beeton's *The Book of Household Management.* Many nineteenth century printed marmalade recipes do seem surprisingly old-fashioned, and it is likely that people often followed the recipes used in their families or by friends, rather than the published cookery-books, when making marmalade. But Scotland was certainly ahead of England in producing a less thick and sticky form of the conserve, which may explain why Scottish recipes were so sought-after among the English in the nineteenth century. Hannah Robertson, as early as the 1760s, had advocated a pint of water to a pound of sugar and a pound of oranges (though a small amount of water may have been lost in clarifying the sugar) in *The Young Ladies School of Arts,* first published in Edinburgh in 1766. [See R 16.] This somewhat less dense and sticky version of marmalade is consonant with its use as a breakfast spread in Scotland at a much earlier date than in England.

The next innovation concerned the pectin in the orange pips. Quince-seeds had long ago been recognised as the source of the gelatinous substance which caused quince marmalade to set. Now that substance was sought in the pips of marmalade oranges. At first they were used rather modestly. In Anne Cobbett's recipe, introduced into the third edition of *The English Housekeeper* in 1842, a wine-pint of water was used for each pound of sugar and pound of fruit-pulp, and the pips were soaked in the water during the time it took to slice the orange-peels. The preserve was then boiled for an hour, which must have taken it well past the optimum setting point of the pectin drawn from the peel and pips. [See R 18.]

A more thorough method for exploiting the pectin in the pips may also have been first devised in Scotland. At any rate, Eliza Acton's 'genuine Scotch marmalade … guaranteed an excellent one by the Scottish lady from whom it was procured', published in 1845, had the orange-pips not merely steeped in water, but then 'well worked with the back of a spoon, a strong clear jelly will be obtained by this means.' Washed off with the steeping water, and passed through a hair-sieve, this liquor was ready to stiffen the marmalade. It contributed to an economical conserve, for now the ratio of ingredients was one pound of oranges and two pounds of sugar to a quart of water (including the steeping water with the jelly of the pips dissolved in it), and the yield of marmalade from the oranges was correspondingly greater. The proportions are those to be found in many standard recipes for Seville orange marmalade today.

The question of whether or not to make marmalade from sweet, China oranges first arose in the eighteenth century when such oranges had only recently ceased to be a novelty. 'Let your Seville oranges be of a light colour, but some make use of China oranges', wrote Mr Borella in 1772 in his recipe for transparent marmalade. Thereafter there are occasional references to sweet oranges in marmalade, often just one or two added to Seville oranges (as in some recipes for 'Scotch marmalade' today); but in Britain they have never offered a serious threat to traditional Seville orange marmalades. The verdict of Thomas Webster's *An Encyclopaedia of Domestic Economy,* 1844, was: 'Common oranges are not equal to the Seville, but they will make very good marmalade.' Such marmalade, blander in flavour than Seville orange marmalade, is also of a cloudier appearance since the rinds and pith of sweet oranges do not boil transparent as those of Seville oranges do. The sweet orange-peels also carry less pectin, but this deficiency can be overcome by adding lemons or lemon-juice and reducing the proportion of water in the marmalade.

One further innovation, which probably took place in the later years of the eighteenth century, was to acquire the aura of a long tradition. This was the use of darker sugar in marmalade-making. When the earlier orange marmalades were prepared in the homes of the well-to-do, the whitest available sugar was called for. The 'double-refined sugar beat fine' suggested by Elizabeth Raffald and others in recipes for transparent marmalade would have helped to produce a pale, clear jelly. But the last decades of the eighteenth century saw a steep rise in the import duties on sugar, leading to increased prices for sugar of all grades. At the same time, marmalade making was moving down the social scale, to be undertaken by people who had to be careful about expense as well as by the wealthier gentry. It was possible to make small savings by using moist, light-brown sugar in jams and marmalades. In dark jams of such fruits as plums or cherries, the appearance was not much affected. The same was true of beaten marmalade, an opaque, orange-coloured, jellied conserve, flecked throughout with tiny fragments of pulp and peel. Its colour was only slightly darkened by the molasses in moist sugar, and the flavour was, to some tastes, enriched.

The confectioners appear to have been quick to grasp the implications in terms of savings to be made. Perhaps the earliest printed reference to moist sugar in this context is in *The Housekeeper's Valuable Present*, c. 1800, where a beaten marmalade recipe begins, 'To a pound of pulp, allow a pound of the best moist sugar.' Richard Abbott, the author, claimed to be 'late apprentice to Messrs Negri and Gunter, Confectioners, in Berkeley Square', so could have learned this usage for moist sugar from his employers.

Thrifty housewives during the nineteenth century continued to use light-brown sugars in marmalade, as it became regular breakfast-time fare and the marmalade-eating habit spread to families on tight budgets. As late as 1916, *A Yorkshire Cookery Book* presented the marmalade recipe of Mrs Riley of Wakefield, which she costed at 4 $^1/_2$ d. a pound if made with white loaf sugar, and 4d. a pound if made with white moist sugar, containing only a little molasses, but fractionally cheaper than refined white sugar. The loaf sugar 'of course is better, but really good results can be obtained with ordinary moist sugar', was Mrs Riley's verdict. As in the case of other confections made with treacle or brown sugar, this type of marmalade was to be singled out as being 'traditional'. When the original beaten orange marmalade was no longer the typical English marmalade, that role was taken over by marmalade darkened with brown sugar or black treacle (molasses); and recipes in this style are still described as Old English marmalade.

MARMALADE MANUFACTURE: THE NINETEENTH-CENTURY EXPANSION

While home-made marmalade recipes proliferated (the Scottish ones acquired a special cachet, sought out by English visitors to Scotland, and by English writers of cookery books), the commercial production of marmalade also expanded steadily. James Keiller's early success encouraged imitators on both sides of the border. Well-made marmalade had good keeping properties and, provided that the large jars into which it was put in the early days were carefully packed, it could travel long distances by land or sea.

Some of the firms involved in the marmalade trade were small, had short lives, and are now forgotten. Descastro & Peach of Piccadilly, Castell & Brown of Princess St, Soho, and W. Hale of Brewer St, Golden Square, were three establishments selling marmalade in London which left a record of their names before they disappeared. Significantly, when samples of their orange marmalades were tested by Arthur Hassall in the 1850s, all contained an excess of copper (a result of over-boiling in unsilvered copper vessels) and one supplied by Castell & Brown held additionally 'a considerable quantity of a vegetable substance, most probably turnip or apple'.[3] Crosse & Blackwell, established in 1830, had also joined the marmalade manufacturers and their versions came out well in Hassall's tests. Another English firm with a familiar name which has been making marmalade since the 1850s is that of W. P. Hartley. But its products did not come to Hassall's notice.[4]

The company of James Robertson & Sons traces its origin to another enterprising Scottish grocer's wife, with a story not unlike that of Janet Keiller. In 1864, James Robertson, a young Paisley grocer, had acquired a barrel of Seville oranges and was unable to sell them. His wife Marion made them up into a transparent jelly marmalade, which she called 'Golden Shred'. It sold very successfully in the Paisley shop, and the Robertsons decided to continue to produce it. Soon their kitchen became too small for the operation, and they opened a factory at Paisley, not far from their grocer's shop.

Four years later, a third Scottish couple embarked on the making and selling of preserves, this time in the far north of Scotland. George Baxter and his wife Margaret set up their grocery business in the village of Fochabers, Morayshire. George Baxter kept the shop and sold the home-made jams and conserves produced by Margaret. Both had previously been in service in Gordon Castle, George as a gardener, and Margaret in the kitchen; and as the family and houseguests of the Duke of Richmond and Gordon had already developed a taste for Margaret's jams and jellies, they had a ready-made clientele. Marmalade may not have been their first product, but since Margaret was able to make it in the early spring, when the local jamming fruits were not available, they soon recognised it as a valuable addition. The members of the family worked hard to enlarge the business, and George and

Margaret's son William used to travel to distant parts of Scotland by train with a supply of her jams and marmalades and his bicycle, so that he could cycle back delivering preserves to customers as he went and collecting new orders.

In the meantime, the firm of James Keiller had prospered. But like all the earliest marmalade-making enterprises, they suffered one particular disadvantage in the high price of sugar, which had carried an import duty in England since 1651, and in Scotland since 1723. Soon after the beginning of the nineteenth century the tax reached a record sum of £8 a hundredweight, but it climbed still further in the next decades and by 1844 it was £8.16s.5d. (£8.82) a hundredweight. The sugar duty may have been one reason for the failure of some smaller marmalade manufacturers of the period, for sugar continued to be taxed, though at a lower and gradually decreasing rate from 1845 until 1874.[5] James Keiller & Son escaped part of the burden by setting up a second manufactory on the island of Guernsey in 1846, under the supervision of Janet's grandson, William, while his brother Alexander looked after the Dundee operation. After the repeal of the sugar duty in 1874 marmalade production was moved from Guernsey to a new Thameside factory at Silvertown, east of the City of London. At Dundee the company had already expanded beyond marmalade, into the fields of bakery and confectionery.

Keiller, Robertson and Baxters are still well-known names in marmalade production, but only Baxters now continue in Scotland. James Robertson & Sons removed to Droylsden, Manchester, many years ago; and since 1988 Keiller marmalade has also been produced at Robertson's Droylsden factory.

Several of today's English marmalade firms, too, began their history during Queen Victoria's reign. Frank Cooper's Oxford marmalade was first sold in 1874 in his shop in Oxford at 84, The High. Once more the pattern was of a husband who was a grocer and his wife, Sarah Jane, who made up marmalade, initially in the kitchens of the Old Angel Hotel, for Frank to sell in his shop. The source of her distinctive recipe may well have been her mother in Bristol; and that is the view held by the firm today. But F. Marian McNeill offered an alternative story:

> About the year 1870 (so the present writer was informed by an Oxford lady, the daughter of an historian of the city who had known the Cooper family) a recipe was brought from a Perthshire manse by an Oxford don, and presented to Mrs Cooper, the wife of a well-known grocer in the city. She placed a few pots of the novelty on her husband's counter, and so popular did it prove among the undergraduates, at whose breakfasts it figured as "squish", that the kitchen soon had to be abandoned for the factory.[6]

Whatever its source, the recipe begins in a unique manner, for a commercially-produced marmalade, in that the oranges are first

Employees at F. Duerr & Son, 1910.

of all boiled whole. At a later stage, when the cut peel and orange hearts have been cooked together they are left to mature for not less than three months, and sometimes for as long as twelve. These and other processes yielded a coarse-cut, aromatic marmalade, which became a favourite among the Oxford dons and undergraduates. Frank Cooper's business expanded rapidly and in 1903 he established a large new marmalade factory opposite Oxford railway station where it formed a landmark for all visitors to the city.

Fred and Mary Duerr founded their jam- and marmalade-making business in Heywood, Lancashire, in 1881. Mary prepared the preserves in her kitchen using her own family recipes, while Fred delivered the filled jars by handcart to the local Co-operative Society and other shops. In 1884 production was moved into a factory building at Guide Bridge, North Manchester; but the business expanded so rapidly that in 1890 Fred commissioned a new model jam and marmalade factory at Old Trafford. The site there is still occupied by Duerr's, now under the direction of Fred and Mary's great-grandson and his two sons.

Some of the English marmalade manufacturers of the later nine-teenth century could well be called orchard firms, not, of course, on the grounds of their ability to raise their own oranges and lemons (for these can never be grown successfully on an orchard scale in Britain); but because they were successful growers of other fruits from which they made jams and preserves, and therefore they had the equipment and the spare capacity in the winter months to undertake the production of orange marmalade.

Chivers of Histon, Cambridgeshire, were a farming family who turned to fruit-farming at a time when corn prices were severely depressed. After Histon had acquired its own railway station they began to send quantities of fruit to the industrial towns of the north of England and eventually William and John, the two sons of Stephen Chivers, set up a wholesale depot at Bradford in Yorkshire to market the fruit on its arrival. Their best customers proved to be jam manufacturers, so they urged their father to try jam-making on the home-ground. With the help of some cooks borrowed from Pembroke College, Cambridge, Chivers made and sold their first jams in 1873, and the next year they constructed a sizable factory, fitted with a steam boiler plant and modern equipment. Before long they coupled marmalade-making with jam production, and their Seville orange marmalade appeared in a price-list of 1877. When they introduced their thick-cut Olde English marmalade in 1907, marketing it as 'The Aristocrat of the Breakfast Table', it proved a great success; and it is still a leading brand today.

Another fruit-farmer, Arthur Wilkin of Tiptree, near Colchester, Essex, embarked on jam manufacture in 1885, influenced by a speech made by the prime minister, Mr Gladstone, who commended fruit-growing and jam-making to his tenants. Arthur Wilkin's venture prospered, and soon afterwards his company added orange marmalade to their jams. Mr C. J. Wilkin, son of Arthur, spent long periods in Jamaica, the United States and Australia between 1890 and 1901 and as a result the company introduced lime, tangerine and grapefruit marmalades into their range at a very early date. Price-lists from the beginning of the twentieth century show that they were then offering for sale no fewer than 27 kinds of marmalade.

A third fruit-grower was Sir Walter Gilbey, of Elsenham Hall near the Essex-Hertfordshire border. He had jams prepared by his cooks from the fruits grown in his gardens and he first presented them for sale in 1890. Within a few months his cooks also began to make both fine-cut and coarse-cut orange marmalades, which were also marketed. The high-quality preserves were a commercial success, and Elsenham jams and marmalades are still produced by methods which have hardly changed over more than a century.

The firm of Moorhouse first made marmalade about 1900, and their marmalades and other preserves have their widest appeal in the north of England. L. Rose and Company is an example of a

Boiling room at Tiptree, 1921.

partnership which had become prominent in another field before it embarked upon marmalade production. The field was, of course, the importation and marketing of bottled lime-juice. Rose's lime marmalade, first produced in the 1930s, was an offshoot of this well-established trade.

In the early days of commercially-produced marmalade, firms such as Crosse & Blackwell had their own shops as outlets for their foodstuffs, including marmalades. Conversely there were certain shops which acquired foodstuffs from a variety of sources, but sold them under their own names. Such a one was Fortnum & Mason, vendors of marmalades for a great many years. Crates of preserved luxury foods from Fortnum & Mason were sent out to the officers who served in the Crimean War, and it is very likely that jars of marmalade were included among the contents.

The growth of all these firms and of others not here mentioned reflects the constant rise in marmalade consumption over the period, not only in the British Isles but also in many overseas countries associated with Britain. Marmalade has proved an excellent article for overseas trade. The high proportion of sugar in its composition is a valuable preservative. Throughout Queen Victoria's reign and thereafter, marmalade, well-sealed in its glazed earthenware or stoneware jars or later in tinned cans, travelled successfully over long distances and proved itself capable of withstanding extremes of temperature. During the nineteenth century orange marmalade became one of the national foods of the British Isles and of English-speaking people throughout the world whose diet was rooted in the British food tradition.

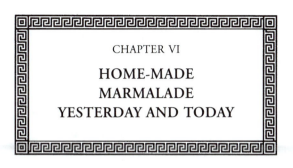

CHAPTER VI

HOME-MADE MARMALADE YESTERDAY AND TODAY

SEVILLE ORANGE MARMALADE

The basic principle of marmalade preparation is so simple – the dividing of the orange into its components, which are separately boiled for appropriate lengths of time before being reboiled with sugar until jelling point is reached – that one might expect the operation to be contained within a single recipe, with no more than two or three variant versions. In fact, an amazing number of combinations and permutations have been developed for each stage. Is the peel to be stripped off and cut up at the beginning, or is it to be boiled, still attached to the pulp of the halved or quartered or occasionally whole oranges, and shredded or chipped when already softened? Is the juice to be squeezed out, held on one side, and added to the rest only at the last boiling? And what about the pulp? Is it to be included? Is it to be used during the preparation of the conserve (as it often is for jelly marmalade, when it is suspended in a muslin bag along with the pips) and then removed and discarded? Or is it to be part of the marmalade? Or is it to be discarded from the start? Recipes can be found to advocate each of these processes in combination with some of the others, based on anything from three oranges (approximately a pound) to several pounds of fruit.

It would be a thankless task to try to analyse even a proportion of the numerous recipes of the past 150 years. But it is interesting to take note of some of the changes that have taken place in marmalade-making procedures in that time.

The initial harvesting of the Seville oranges in Spain has moved back earlier in the year. Mrs Beeton wrote in 1861 that orange marmalade 'should be made in March or April, as Seville oranges are then in perfection.' Her contemporary, Anne Bowman, put the marmalade-making season 'about February or March, when the Seville oranges are plentiful and in the best condition.' *Harmsworth's Household Encyclopaedia* of 1923 echoes Anne Bowman, saying, 'February and March are the seasons when marmalade is usually made, as Seville oranges are then plentiful and cheap.' Today the season is at its height in the second half of January, and those who wait into February may find that the Seville oranges have already disappeared from their greengrocers' displays.

The fruits we receive today are actually less mature than those preserved by earlier generations. The skins of Seville oranges thicken as the season advances, and the proportion of skin to pulp and juice becomes higher. Since much of the pectin of the bitter orange is stored in the white peel behind the orange surface, late-season orange-peel supplied more pectin and increased the setting quality of the marmalade. But it was also more difficult and time-consuming to cut up. Today we add extra pectin to marmalade by extracting it from the pips, either pre-soaking them and adding their water, or tying them up in a muslin bag to hang in the preserving pan while the pulp and peel boil together. And we are able to incorporate more water into our recipes as a result, and to produce more marmalade.

It is pectin which gives stability to the set of all marmalades and jams. Chemically, pectin is composed of long thread-like molecules and, during gel formation, these molecules link loosely together into a three-dimensional network. In marmalade-making, the preliminary boiling or soaking of the pips, pith, and peel releases the pectin but its setting property is activated only when it is combined with sugar and fruit acid during the final stage of marmalade-boiling. Even then the balance is not always an easy one to achieve, for too much acid can produce a rapid set and then cause the jelly to split easily so that sugary syrup 'weeps' from it; while too little acid delays setting, or even prevents it altogether. Again, too much sugar or over-cooking the preserve can make marmalade crystallise during storage, while with too little sugar or with under-cooking the set is syrupy or the marmalade may begin to ferment or to collect moulds.

During the earlier part of the nineteenth century, beaten marmalade was still being made. As an alternative to chip marmalade it was gradually superseded by the clear jelly marmalades. These grew out of the eighteenth-century transparent marmalades with their clear shreds of Seville orange peel no less than did chip marmalade. Margaret Dods in 1826 published a recipe for a peel-less transparent marmalade made only from the fruit-pulp, washed in a little water and strained, plus the juice and a pound of sugar to each pint of liquid. 'Use the skins for candied peel', she suggested. Today the name given to this conserve is jelly marmalade, and it is stiffened with pectin extracted from the orange-pips and also from the finely-shredded peel. For both orange and grapefruit jelly marmalades lemon-juice is also added at the final boiling of the liquid with sugar, to assist the set.

For chunky marmalade the preparation of the peel can be a tedious job. Formerly, when beaten marmalade was made the skins were always boiled soft before being submitted to the pestle and mortar. In the case of chip or shred marmalades practice varied, the orange-peel being pre-boiled before it was sliced in some cases but not in others. The commercial marmalade producers were the first to seek ways of speeding up the work. Keiller's records show that Wedderspoon Keiller, younger brother of the James who founded the firm, designed a machine to cut up orange-peel at the Dundee factory. The invention of the mincing machine in the mid-nineteenth century brought relief to some home marmalade-makers (though minced peel does not have the attractive appearance of finely-cut peel). But in due course the purpose-built marmalade-cutter was devised and was a useful tool in households where marmalade was made on a considerable scale.[1] Today the home marmalade-maker can slice up the peel quickly and effortlessly with the help of an electric food-mixer; and men often like to take over this part of marmalade preparation.

The bitterness of the orange-peels troubled the early marmalade-makers. Not only were the oranges pre-soaked and boiled in changes of water, but in some recipes they were also rubbed with salt or left overnight in brine. This practice has been abandoned today by home marmalade-makers. But a few commercial firms still soak the oranges in brine, afterwards thoroughly washed off, so as to soften the peel and reduce boiling time.

Not much is said in the early cookery-books about any preliminary cleaning of the oranges, perhaps because they were so thoroughly soaked and boiled before marmalade-making began. Mrs Frazer in 1791 introduced her recipe, rather exceptionally, with the words, 'Weigh the oranges ... wipe all the oranges with a wet cloth to take off the blackness, and grate them.'

Today citrus fruits arrive in Britain with their skins painted with vegetable oil or preservative wax to prevent mould or insect infestation during their journey. The first task of today's marmalade-maker is to scrub the oranges, lemons or grapefruits thoroughly in water so that no extraneous flavour can taint the finished marmalade.

Marmalade-cutter.
Harmsworth's Household Encyclopaedia, vol. 3, 1923.

MARMALADES OF CITRUS FRUITS OTHER THAN ORANGES

Lemons are occasionally named in the earlier orange marmalade recipes, not as a supplement to oranges, but as a marmalade fruit in their own right. Sir Hugh Plat in 1605 offered a recipe for the old, solid, slicing marmalade made with either 10 lemons or 10 Seville oranges, boiled and sieved with half a dozen pippins. [See R 11.] Lemons rarely received marmalade recipes in their own right; more often the instruction 'Thus also may you make marmalade of lemons' followed an orange marmalade recipe. But in a few cases the reverse was true. [See R 13.]

Mrs Rundell recommended both orange and lemon marmalades as 'very good and elegant sweetmeats' and so they may have been in some English circles. Scottish experience was evidently different, and Margaret Dods in the 1820s said that lemon marmalade 'is seldom seen'. But it became better known generally later in the century. It is an ingredient in the celebrated Snowdon pudding recorded by Eliza Acton in 1855. Marmalade manufacturers began to sell it, on a modest scale. It was on Crosse & Blackwell's price-list of 1884 as a speciality in 1 lb. fluted jars (whereas orange marmalade was sold in several sizes and containers graded from 1 lb. to 14 lb. weight). Today its recipes are found regularly side by side with those for orange marmalade. Lemon marmalade has a tangy, attractive flavour and gives two great advantages to the home marmalade-maker. It can be made at any time, for lemons are imported all through the year; and it always sets well, because the juice, as well as the peel of lemons, is rich in pectin and acid.

Commercial manufacturers such as Wilkin of Tiptree first introduced marmalades of other citrus fruits to Britain. Such marmalades were already being made in some countries where the fruits were grown. The West Indies was one such region. Limes had been naturalised in several West Indian islands long ago by the

Spanish, and their expressed juice began to be shipped from there to Europe as early as the 1680s. The West Indies was also the home of the grapefruit, which emerged there, probably in Jamaica, in the eighteenth century. It was either a sport of the large, thick-skinned shaddock, sometimes called pomelo, or a cross between that fruit and a sweet orange. The mandarin or tangerine orange, by contrast, came to Europe direct from its home in China and the earliest tree to arrive was brought to England in 1 805. It became the progenitor of trees which were established in Malta, and from there the mandarin was introduced into Sicily and Italy.[2]

These citrus fruits began to be imported into Britain in the late nineteenth century, though on no great scale. The 1911 edition of the *Encyclopaedia Britannica* referred to the export of lime fruits from the West Indies as a recent development, compared with the long-established trade in lime-juice, adding that 'Limalade, or pre-

17th-century lemon. *A Book of Fruits & Flowers*, 1653.

[87]

served limes, is an excellent substitute for marmalade.' It seems that commercial producers of marmalade, such as Wilkin of Tiptree, were the first to use limes for that purpose, and housewives, even when they were able to buy lime-fruits in the shops, did not at once follow suit. Instead of making them into marmalade they preserved the fruits whole in syrup, at least during the period before the 1914–18 war. May Byron in her *Jam Book* (1917) gave a recipe for the syrup for whole limes but claimed that they were not, at that time, used to make jam, marmalade or jelly.

Grapefruits were incorporated more readily into marmalade-making. May Byron offered two recipes for marmalades of grapefruits alone, a third which combined four grapefruits with six oranges, and another for grapefruit jelly. She also gave instructions for making four different tangerine marmalades, one including lemons. In Britain's markets today, tangerines or mandarins have almost been superseded by satsumas, of the same family but pipless, or with few pips, in contrast to the very pippy tangerines. From the marmalade-maker's point of view, satsumas are somewhat less flavourful than tangerines, and of course do not yield the amount of pectin which was previously to be obtained from tangerine pips.

WARTIME AND POST-WAR MARMALADE

May Byron's book gives little hint of the problems of marmalade-making in wartime, yet they must have been considerable. Before the 1914–18 war much of the sugar eaten in Britain was cane sugar which came mainly from the West Indies. During the war, merchant shipping was at risk from enemy action, and the British Government deeply regretted that it had not followed the example of many European countries and developed a sugar-beet industry within Britain. Frequent shortages of both imported sugar and citrus fruits inevitably curbed marmalade-making during the period of the war. Afterwards, in the 1920s, encouragement was given to sugar-beet growers, and home-produced beet sugar has been available in Britain ever since. It was to prove a great standby at the time of the 1939–45 war.

During that second world war, merchant shipping again faced great dangers in order to bring in essential foodstuffs. Sugar was not plentiful, but at least was rationed on a fair basis of $1/2$ lb. a person each week, and careful families could put by enough for occasional small-scale jam or marmalade-making. Citrus fruits were not among the most essential imports but they were a great morale-booster. On the rare occasions when a cargo of sweet oranges arrived at a British port, they too were distributed scrupulously through the country. Housewives queued for hours at their green-grocers' to receive eventually a single pound (three oranges). At home, when the fruit had been enjoyed, the skins were not discarded. Chopped and boiled, they became the basis of mar-malades made with apples and some of the hoarded sugar, with bitterness supplied by quassia chips bought from the chemist.

Bananas were even rarer than oranges, and were also patiently queued for by housewives. At least one small child, given her first banana to take and show to friends at school, carefully brought the blackened skin home in her purse in the belief that it, too, could be made into marmalade.

In the post-war years, Seville oranges have once more been ob-tainable and an increasing variety of other citrus fruits has reached the markets and shops. Ambitious marmalade-makers in Britain can find in the larger supermarkets nowadays limes, cumquats, pomelos, ortaniques, minneolas, and ugli-fruits. The ugli-fruit is one of the tangelos, hybrids bred by crossing tangerines with grape-fruits. Other new citrus hybrids are bred from time to time. Not all prove suitable for marketing, but we can certainly expect to see further novel citrus fruits available for marmalade-making in the years to come.

Those who are pressed for time can nowadays rely on canned prepared marmalade pulps. Citrus peel and pulp, when they have had their preliminary boiling together, can be sealed and stored for very long periods provided air is excluded; and the makers of the canned prepared pulps have been able to take advantage of this characteristic. All that is required, when the can is opened, is for the contents to be mixed with sugar and water in appropriate proportions, boiled for a short time, and then potted up. One advantage is that Seville orange marmalade can be made at any time of year. More recently frozen prepared peel-and-pulp has also become available.

The home freezer can be useful to those who wish to postpone their marmalade-making. Freshly bought citrus fruits can be frozen whole, if they are first well scrubbed in water, then dried and packed in polythene bags. Alternatively they can be cut up and cooked through the first stage until the peel is tender; then the peel-and-pulp mixture can be put into containers and frozen. After thawing, it will require only the final boiling with sugar. But it is advisable to use extra fruit (one-eighth more than the recipe specifies), or to add lemon-juice, to offset the pectin loss caused by freezing.

The pressure-cooker can also save the time of the marmalade-maker. The preliminary boiling of the peel (under pressure) should not take more than fifteen minutes, after which the closed pan must be left to cool for at least ten minutes to allow the pressure to drop before the lid is removed. For the second boiling with sugar either the pressure-cooker without its lid or an open preserving pan can be used, and this stage should not take more than twenty to twenty-five minutes. We may no longer have handmaids to help us to prepare our marmalade, as our Tudor and Stuart and Georgian forebears did, but our task has been considerably eased by the time- and energy-saving equipment available for the home today.

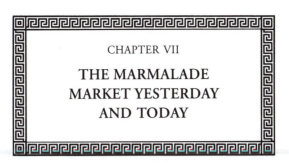

STANDARDS AND VARIETIES

Until the late 1960s, the market in Britain for factory-made marmalade was buoyant. The usual British cooked breakfast of fried bacon and eggs, or sausage and bacon, or boiled or scrambled eggs, or haddock, or kippers, preceded by porridge or cereal, was completed with toast or bread and marmalade. Those who did not consume a cooked breakfast nevertheless often breakfasted on toast and marmalade, with an extra 'course' supplied by fruit or fruit-juice. Many people enjoyed home-made marmalade, but others were happy to rely on the manufactured marmalades they could purchase from their grocers, marmalades which, during the twentieth century, have been made to very high standards.

Standards have not always been so reliable. Food adulteration had become a huge problem by the middle years of the nineteenth century, eventually mitigated by the 1872 Adulteration of Food, Drink and Drugs Act, and the 1875 Sale of Food and Drugs Act. Those Acts were steered through Parliament only after years of campaigning by the food quality reformers. One of them, Arthur Hassall, published the results of his chemical analyses of processed foods of every kind in two books titled *Food and its Adulterations* and *Adulterations Detected.*

His comments on marmalade are revealing. In the earlier book he wrote, 'There is no doubt but that some of what professes to be real "Scotch marmalade" consists of a mixture of sweet and bitter oranges, if indeed inferior ingredients do not partly compose it.'[1] In *Adulterations Detected* he expanded on the theme: 'Orange marmalade, which, when genuine, consists only of the bitter or Seville orange, is frequently adulterated with sweet oranges, with apples and turnips. We have been informed that a species of swede of a yellow colour is much used in the adulteration of orange marmalade. Lastly, we have good authority for stating that partly-decayed oranges and even sucked oranges are used in the adulteration of this favourite preserve; these statements rest upon the authority of an eye-witness ... There is a kind of turnip, the seeds of which are frequently advertised in the "Gardener's Chronicle" for sale, of a yellow colour, and which is called the orange turnip. We know not to what use this can be put unless in the adulteration of orange marmalade.'[2]

In his analysis of nineteen marmalade samples, most supplied by shops which have long since disappeared, several contained excessive amounts of copper, and 'these were adulterated with large quantities of a vegetable substance, most probably turnip or apple'. It is interesting that apples, which had been acceptable in home-made marmalades in the seventeenth century, and sweet oranges, sometimes added to them in the eighteenth, were regarded by Hassall as adulterants.

Fly-by-night firms of the period also tried to turn the success of Keiller's Dundee marmalade to their advantage. 'It is needful to speak ... cautiously of the marmalade of commerce', wrote J. C. Jeaffreson, 'because the omnipresent Dundee marmalade contains a large proportion of boiled carrot, a vegetable whose sweetness spares the manufacturer's sugar-barrel, and whose mild flavour is lost in that of almost any fruit with which it is combined. A very palatable carrot marmalade may be made of boiled carrots, mashed and seasoned with a little lemon-peel and lemonjuice.'[3]

In contrast to the producers of such inferior marmalades were those other firms whose reputation grew because of the fine quality of their preserves.[4] Many of today's marmalade manufacturers can trace their history back to Queen Victoria's reign and some of the marmalades produced then, such as Robertson's Golden and Silver Shred, and Cooper's Oxford, have hardly changed since because the characteristics through which they appealed to nineteenth-century consumers are still attractive to us today.[5] Other firms have introduced their most popular marmalades during the present century. Marmalade was in its heyday in the Edwardian era. It was then that Wilkin of Tiptree were issuing price-lists describing no fewer than 27 marmalades, which must have included several different kinds of Seville orange marmalade as well as those of other citrus fruits (and doubtless a few of the traditional non-citrus marmalades, such as apricot, peach and quince). Today fifteen different Tiptree marmalades are produced, twelve of them based wholly or partly on Seville oranges. Lemon, lime and grapefruit marmalades are also made, but are less popular than the orange varieties.

Chivers Olde English, a coarse-cut orange marmalade introduced in 1907, was followed by other new marmalades. Chivers' price-lists of the 1930s show an orange marmalade with fine-cut peel, an orange jelly marmalade, and also grapefruit (1932 or earlier), lime, and ginger marmalades. Rose's lime marmalade likewise originated in the inter-war years. Robertson added thick-cut orange marmalade to their Golden and Silver Shred, and later introduced both ginger and lime marmalades. In an advertisement of 1925, Hartley offered three different orange marmalades – Seville star, coarse-cut and jelly – and also ginger marmalade.

Ginger marmalade is something of an anomaly, as ginger is the only root to be incorporated in a conserve in recognisable chunks for the sake of its distinctive taste (carrots appear in some home-made marmalade recipes, but are present chiefly to give bulk and sweetness, and their flavour is masked by citrus fruit peel and juice). Ginger marmalade has been made and sold by several manufac-turers over a number of years; and, since the ginger-chunks are similar in consistency to chips of citrus fruit peel, consumers have never questioned its role as a marmalade. Nevertheless, it is not a true marmalade, since it requires the addition of pectin from an outside source – usually apple jelly or commercial pectin. This factor has been the cause of the change in its name brought about by current EEC regulations. The commercially-produced conserve formerly on the market under the name 'ginger marmalade' now has to appear in the shops labelled 'ginger jam' or 'ginger preserve'.

Thus the invention and marketing of new citrus fruit mar-malades, and the creation of ginger-root marmalades, were well under way in the first decades of this century. With the end of food rationing after the 1939–45 war, the trend continued. Rose's three-fruit conserve of orange, lime and grapefruit was launched in the 1950s under the name 'West Indian marmalade'; it was later rechristened 'Select orange marmalade'. In the mid-1960s Rose's earlier lime marmalade was joined by a lime and lemon marmalade and in 1968 they introduced tangerine marmalade.

Keiller's marketed a jelly marmalade alongside their long-established Dundee marmalade for many years, and in the early 1970s introduced rough-cut lemon, chunky grapefruit and three-fruits marmalades. Elsenham Quality Foods, having sold orange marmalade since 1890, added marmalades of other citrus fruits in 1967. Their range now contains seven different orange mar-malades, including a vintage one, two fortified with alcohol, and an orange and ginger, as well as their grapefruit; lime and lemon; tangerine; and three-fruits marmalades. Hartley, who had been producing orange marmalade since the 1850s, diversified into marmalades of other fruits only after the firm, which was taken over by Schweppes in 1959, had become part of Cadbury Schweppes ten years later. Fortnum & Mason currently offer no fewer than nineteen different marmalades, some traditional, other reflecting the modern trend towards unusual combinations (for example, their Seville orange and peach), and today's wider range of citrus fruits (for example, their cumquat; their blood orange; and their pink grapefruit marmalades). Sold under Fortnum's label, these preserves are made up for them and to their own recipes by well-established specialist marmalade-manufacturers.

Frank Cooper have continued to concentrate upon the Oxford marmalade for which they have been famed since 1874; but whereas their operation used to take place entirely within the fine new manufactory built in 1903 opposite Oxford's railway station, by the 1960s output had increased to such an extent that the firm transferred the earlier stages of production to premises in Andalucia

Delivery-van from Robertson's Bristol factory, c.1914.

in Spain, home of the Seville oranges used for the marmalade. Nowadays no part of the operation is carried out in Oxford, and the factory facing the station has been put to other purposes.

Throughout Britain a number of small private enterprises are engaged in marmalade production. Their methods are closer to those of the home marmalade-maker than those of the purpose-built factories, and thus far more time-consuming, which has to be reflected in the price of the product. Their jars of marmalade are displayed and sold in local delicatessens and gift-shops, often very successfully. But success brings its own problems, with the small-scale entrepreneur facing demands for output and marketing far beyond the range of a cottage industry. At that point he or she may well decide to become a subsidiary of a much larger food corporation.

But in addition to the output of the small-scale producers and of the well-known companies mentioned in this book, a very large quantity of marmalade, made from all the principal citrus fruits, alone or in combination, retails under the 'own label' brands of the big supermarket chains. Although such marmalades have to con-form to the same regulations concerning percentages of fruit and sugar as do all others, they tend to be blander and less distinctive than those produced by the smaller specialist firms. But they are also cheaper. So they appeal to the majority of consumers, that is to families or individuals on a fairly tight budget who are content with a pleasant, sweet, slightly tangy conserve, even if it is rather less flavourful than some of its more expensive counterparts. The days when cheaper marmalades were likely to be diluted with carrots or turnips are long since past. The legislation which in 1872 and 1875 made food adulterations illegal has been further streng-thened by new Acts passed during this century. Public analysts were first appointed to counties and boroughs in 1872, and have been at hand throughout the present century to check and test any doubtful samples of foodstuffs. As a final safeguard all labels on marmalade-jars now have to state the percentage of sugar and fruit in the contents, as well as mentioning whether any additional pectin, or the recently permitted preservatives are present. Those who buy 'own brand' marmalades from their supermarkets will obtain a reliable preserve manufactured under strict quality controls.

VINTAGE AND LIQUEUR MARMALADES

Among the newer marmalades now available, two types may be singled out. The first is vintage marmalade. Mr Anthony J. G. Blunt, former owner of Elsenham, reported that when he bought the firm in 1959 he found some pre-war 2 lb. jars of thick-cut marmalade, then at least twenty years old. When he tasted it he found it 'positively ambrosial, proving to his complete satisfaction that marmalade really does improve with age.'[6] The idea that marmalade can be mellowed by maturing the pulp and peel after they have been boiled together for the first time is not new. Frank Cooper's Oxford marmalade was traditionally matured at pulp stage for three months and sometimes for as long as twelve. But, as Anthony Blunt found out, a similar improvement can take place too when the completed marmalade remains sealed in its jar, as the chunks of peel slowly soften and release their full flavour into the marmalade while its sugar content continues to protect it. Today several firms sell special vintage marmalades. Among them are Elsenham's Vintage Orange and Fortnum & Mason's Sir Nigel's Vintage Orange.

The second newer range is that of the liqueur marmalades. Baxters appear to have been first in the field with their whisky marmalade, which chimes in well with their general objective of preserving and marketing Scottish Highland produce. Exhaustive experiments were made in order to find a satisfactory way of combining the whisky of north-east Scotland with Seville orange marmalade made to Baxters' own recipes. The product was

THE BOOK OF MARMALADE

matured in Speyside whisky casks for five years and in 1952 was put on the market. It was so successful that its manufacture has continued ever since.

Elsenham have also entered the liqueur marmalade market. Anthony Blunt in the early 1960s began to consider the possibility of adding brandy to Elsenham marmalade by some process analogous to the Swiss practice of floating a layer of kirsch over cherry conserve. After a number of experiments the method was perfected. But the first experiment was the most startling and Mr Blunt was generous enough to send me an account of what happened. This is the story, in his own words:

> One day, the jam-boiling team was assembled in the then small and low-ceilinged Boiling Room, and the marmalade fruit and sugar were prepared. At the last minute, Blunt poured into the pans several bottles of Brandy. All the small staff gathered round to watch the experiment. The resultant mixture was then potted off amidst a certain amount of excited merriment. The next batch was then prepared and, wincing at the cost of the trial, Blunt added several bottles of Whisky. The air was redolent with fumes of oranges and alcohol. By this time the first batch with Brandy was just cool enough to taste. With much giggling, everyone tried it. Sadly, no-one could detect any difference. Surprisingly, there was no despondency, but a carefree willingness to try again, using *more* liqueur.
>
> Again and again the experiment was repeated. More and more precious bottles went into the boiling pans. The noise levels grew. Red faces shone in the steam. More and more batches and more and more alcohol were boiled up. Blunt suddenly realised that not only had he run out of drink, but all the staff were behaving most peculiarly. They were – not to put too fine a point on it – Drunk!

The next morning, a sombre and rather the worse for wear crew arrived for the tasting – absolutely no difference to the product from ordinary marmalade, only hangovers for the dejected team. Slowly he realised that all the alcohol had volatilised.

Later experiments were on a smaller scale and more carefully controlled, with the fruit marinated in the spirits; and Elsenham liqueur marmalade and other liqueur preserves went into production in 1962. Their popularity, especially as gifts in the Christmas season, may be judged by the fact that Elsenham in the 1980s produced a brandy marmalade, a rum marmalade, two whisky marmalades (one a vintage marmalade with Glenfiddich, still marketed today), and orange ginger marmalade with ginger wine. For Christmas 1982 Elsenham launched 'The English gentleman's special reserve marmalade' in the form of a pack containing two half-pound jars of brandy marmalade, made with extra Seville orange peel and French brandy, together with the suggestion that one should be eaten straight away, while the other was laid down, when it 'will keep on improving in the jar until the end of the century, as the liquor permeates the peel of the bitter Seville oranges'. Former recipients who have succeeded in keeping the second jar intact through the years will be able to test this claim at their first breakfast of the new millennium.

Duerr's brought out their orange with whisky 'Signature marmalade' in August 1997 to celebrate the achievement of their billionth jar of marmalade since the first was put on sale in 1881. Today, Fortnum & Mason offer a choice of thin-cut orange marmalades fortified with one of three alcoholic liqueurs: champagne, Cointreau or whisky. Wilkin's fine-cut orange and malt whisky marmalade was introduced a few years ago as a seasonal line for Christmas, but then went on to sell steadily through the year.

PRODUCTION AND MARKETING

The preparation of liqueur marmalades is clearly no easy business. But even in the production of ordinary citrus marmalades, there are variations in practice. Some are due to the scale on which the marmalade is made and others to the type produced, since the process for jelly marmalades differs from that for thick-cut chunky ones. The smaller firms, such as Baxters, Wilkin of Tiptree, and Elsenham, prefer open copper pans, nowadays well silvered to prevent the copper contaminating the preserve. Copper conducts heat quickly and evenly, and the boiling in open pans helps to invert the sugar properly so that it cannot recrystallise. The fifth and final boiling of Frank Cooper's Oxford marmalade is also carried out in open pans for that reason.

But other firms, working on a large scale, favour steaming the fruit. Chivers, who originally used massive silvered copper pans, had replaced them before 1939 with huge steel vats, in which fruits for jam- and marmalade-making can be boiled very quickly at high temperatures. Robertson's carry out their final boiling for their Golden Shred in pot-bellied closed copper boiling pans. As the jelly begins to cool, the orange shreds are distributed evenly through it, and it then enters into a high-speed bottling plant where it is quickly measured into glass jars, capped and sealed; and after being cooled off and labelled, it is ready for the customer.

Many manufacturers nowadays begin their marmalade pre-paration in Spain, where the oranges are harvested. In 1990, Henrietta Green reported that 90 per cent of Britain marmalade was made from imported pulp.[7] So it is in Spain that the hearts and peels of the majority of marmalade oranges are separated; and the peels are shredded to the prescribed size by mechanical cutters, and tenderised by boiling or steaming, and soaked in syrup before being re-united with the pre-cooked and sieved inner part of the fruit.

The pulp is then sealed in tins and pasteurised, or alternatively is put into cartons and protected by an injection of sulphur dioxide; and it is then ready to be transported to Britain. There, the pulp is reboiled with pectin and sugar, the sulphur dioxide being driven off at an early stage by the boiling process. The final phase of marmalade preparation is very similar to jam-making; and most of the large-scale commercial firms producing marmalade do in fact use their equipment to make soft-fruit jams at the appropriate times of the year.

Jelly marmalades are made with the juice extracted from the citrus fruits. Again, the extraction and concentration of the juice is most often carried out in the countries where the fruits are grown. The degree of concentration of the juice is carefully assessed because the amount of fruit content required for different types of marmalade is specified under regulations prescribed in United Kingdom and European Union law. Marmalade must contain a

13 Orange Marmalade, &c.

Orange Marmalade,	1 lb. fluted pots	...	4/6
„	„	2 lb. glass jars	......	8/-
„	„	3 lb. glass jars	......	11/3
„	„	4 lb. tins	....	16/-
„	„	4 lb. brown jars	......	18/-
Lemon Marmalade, fluted pots	....	..	5/-
Quince	„	glass jars	....	9/-

½d. per lb. extra for quantities of less than 144 lbs.

| Orange Marmalade in 7 lb. | } | per lb. | ... | 3½d. |
| and 14 lb. tins or jars | ... | } | per cwt.... | 30/- |

7 & 14 lb. Tins charged 2d. and 4d. each are not returnable.
  „   Jars charged 6d. and 9d. each are returnable.
Crates containing 1 cwt. Marmalade in Tins are charged 6d. each, not retnrnable.

Crosse & Blackwell's price-list, August 1884.
Prices given are for one dozen jars.

minimum of 20 grams of citrus fruit per 100 grams, or which 7.5 grams or more is derived from the centre of the fruit. 'Extra fruit' marmalade of course contains more: the amount must be stated on the jar label.

All marmalade manufacturers, whether using open copper pans or closed boilers, carry out the operation as speedily as possible, so as to retain the flavour. And some of the specialist makers improve their preserve by periods of maturation between the first and second boiling of the ingredients. In commercially-produced marmalades, sugar is often added in the form of 'a filtered syrup of known strength, instead of dry sugar, the best of which may contain specks of insoluble matter, which mar the appearance of the product.'[8]

The packaging and labelling of marmalade is obviously a valuable factor in establishing particular brands and varieties, and in keeping the name of the manufacturer in the public eye. The home-made marmalades of the eighteenth century were stored in glass pots. But James Keiller in their earliest days utilised white stoneware jars, cheaper then than glass, and not quite so fragile, a point to be considered in view of the long journeys, by land and by sea, on which some of the pots were sent.

During the nineteenth century both glass and pottery containers were in use. Where marmalade was packed in quantity – and 7 lb. and 14 lb. were two amounts regularly on sale to cater for the large families and households of the day – the container was always of glazed pottery or stoneware. Later the bigger quantities were often available in tinned cans, hermetically sealed, for the method of preserving meat in sealed cans, perfected earlier in the century, came to be applied to vegetables, fruit, and sweet conserves. Crosse & Blackwell in 1884 sold orange marmalade in 1 lb. fluted pots, 2 lb. and 3 lb. glass jars, 4 lb. brown jars (glazed earthenware), and 7 lb. and 14 lb. jars, unspecified on the price-list for lack of space but doubtless again brown jars. These two large sizes carried a deposit of 6d. (2 $^1/_2$ p) and 9d. (4 p) respectively, and were return-able, so arrangements existed at the factory to sterilise and re-use them.

Pottery and glass jars coexisted for a long time. May Byron in 1917 advised the home jam- and marmalade-maker to have supplies of both at hand. Keiller continued to produce their distinctive printed white stoneware pots through the first half of the twentieth century, though by the 1960s only small numbers were being made for some of the export marmalade; they were specially popular in the United States. The white stoneware jars printed for Frank Cooper with the words 'Frank Cooper's "Oxford" home-made marmalade' were also well-known in their time. The demise of the stoneware jar was due partly to its eventual high cost and partly to the fact that it could not be vacuum-sealed, as glass jars can be, and had to be closed with a parchment cap. This led to a very slight risk of moulds developing on the surface of the marmalade, though that could only have happened if the jar was stored in exceptionally damp surroundings.

Vacuum sealing was pioneered by Fred Duerr as long ago as 1905, and thereafter was gradually adopted by all marmalade manu-facturers, though it was not until the 1950s that glass marmalade and jam jars were universally sealed by this method. More recently, in 1991, Duerr's pioneered the tamper-evident button cap.

Today marmalade is packed in glass jars which display the clear jelly or the thicker, darker pulp. The simple printed labels used by Wilkin of Tiptree and Frank Cooper have a traditional look. Most other firms have produced labels in bright modern colours, often showing the fruits contained in the marmalade. But all jar labels, whatever their design, must now follow EEC regulations and list not only the ingredients of the preserve, but also the proportion of both fruit and sugar per 100 grams.

With so many marmalades to choose from and new ones coming onto the market at no great intervals, consumers should have been happy to continue to purchase them on the same scale as they had done during the first half of the twentieth century. But this has not been the case. The decline in marmalade consumption was already under way during the 1960s. It was due in part to changing food habits. Fewer people now eat a full cooked breakfast; and for some, cereals and muesli have replaced not only bacon and eggs, but also toast and marmalade. More recently, breakfast has disappeared altogether for some younger people who compensate by snacking en route to their work. The solid marmalade suet pudding is not often in evidence; once it would have appeared nearly every week in some households, accompanied by marmalade sauce. As a spread, marmalade faces more competition than formerly from honey and from sweet spreads other than jam. Pricing, too, does not encourage marmalade-buying, with Value Added Tax and the higher cost of fruit and sugar reflected in increasing prices in the shops for both marmalade and jam.

In fact, the market for sweet spreads of all kinds has been shrinking for a long time. The decline in jam consumption has been even more marked than that in marmalade, as families increasingly take their main cooked meal of the day in the evening; and fewer of them eat the type of high tea which calls for a plentiful supply of bread and jam. Jam, however, has recently recovered somewhat from its former unhealthy image linking it with obesity and tooth decay as a result of the new extra-fruit and reduced-sugar versions now on the market; and the rate of decline in its consumption had slowed.

The marmalade-producing firms have continued to experiment with new recipes, especially ones based on citrus fruits other than oranges, Recent examples are Crabtree & Evelyn's coarse-cut satsuma marmalade, and the pink grapefruit marmalades offered by Fortnum & Mason and by Harvey Nichols. EEC legislation adopted in August 1981 made it possible to market marmalades with a sugar content of less than 68.5 per cent which was the minimum permitted in Britain by an earlier Ministry of Food

Standard, in force since 1944. Such marmalades are allowed to contain an additional preservative. A number of firms have introduced sugar-reduced marmalades as a result, though with mixed success.

Wilkin of Tiptree launched two high-fruit, 45 per cent sugar marmalades in the late 1980s, but had to abandon them after three years due to poor sales. James Robertson, after selling their Today's Recipe marmalades with a sugar content of 48 per cent for several years, discontinued production of sugar-reduced types in 1998. But other makers have persevered with sugar-reduced recipes, and their products comprised 4 per cent of the total marmalade market in 1997, proving that such marmalades have become the choice of a significant number of people.[9]

Several manufacturers nowadays offer marmalade in 12 ounce (340 gm.) jars, instead of the long-established one-pound jar. Some vary their sizes for different types of marmalade: eight of Wilkin's marmalades come in 340 gm. jars, and the other seven in 454 gm. (one-pound) jars. The 340 gm. size was adopted quite widely in the belief that its lower cost to consumers would help to cushion the inevitable year by year rise in marmalade prices in the shops. The reasoning behind this innovation seems to have been that since we were by the early 1980s eating less than three-quarters of the amount of marmalade consumed per head in 1960, it followed that we would prefer to buy it in jars only three-quarters of the old one-pound size – not as logical as it may look, since the amount eaten varies enormously from one individual to another.

Nevertheless, a good deal of marmalade is still presented in one-pound jars, and recently some firms have revived the two-pound size, usually only for their strongest-selling marmalade. At the other end of the scale, Duerr's have introduced a quarter-pound (113 gm.) jar for the occasional marmalade user.

Duerr's were also the first to abandon the use of tinned cans as containers for large quantities of marmalade. The traditional seven-pound cans were originally put on the market for families with numerous children and households with many servants, and more recently for institutions and the catering trade. Duerr's introduced large foil-sealed plastic polytubs with tight-fitting lids and carrying-handles in 1985. There were both more hygienic and easier to move around than the metal cans, and similar tubs have since been adopted by other firms engaged in bulk sales.

Another growth area in marmalade packaging has been that of miniatures. The one or one-and-a-half ounce plastic pack represent the single meal size, and is widely utilised by hotel chains and other catering establishments.

Little one-and-a-half ounce (42 gm.) glass jars of marmalade were initially seen most often in a gift context, especially in the weeks before Christmas. Then, assorted marmalades, including liqueur marmalades, appeared in the shops in their small jars boxed together, sometimes along with a packet of breakfast tea. Boxes of miniatures are still a gift item at Christmas. But today the larger supermarkets have stocks of tiny jars of marmalades and jams on their shelves all year round, giving the customer the chance to try out a new brand or a new citrus fruit flavour at little cost, or to offer a selection to visitors at any time.

The smaller specialist makers have also discovered the saleability of their premium marmalades as food presents in full-size twelve-ounce or one-pound jars. An information leaflet issued by Elsenham in the mid-1980s claimed that it was 'as usual to see [their] attractively boxed preserves, teas and other lines in quality gift-shops as it is to see them in department-store food halls and good class grocers.' And the gift role assigned to extra special marmalades certainly continues today.

Many firms both large and small export marmalade overseas, some to more than 40 countries. Though there has been some contraction in the marmalade market in Britain, the export market for marmalade is an expanding one.

It is the smaller firms making high-quality special marmalades who have been least affected by the decline in marmalade-eating in Britain. Their clientele in earlier days was not large. Even during the 1930s, Wilkin and Sons of Tiptree were still supplying marmalades and other preserves to most of their customers direct from the factory, not through shops; and they claim that the names of typical customers of that period were to be 'found in such publications as Crockford's *Clerical Directory* and *Debrett's*.'

Today's decline in marmalade consumption has not been in those circles, but among the low-waged and the unemployed. It is also apparent that the younger members of the population eat less marmalade than do the middle-aged and elderly, a cause for some concern to the manufacturers. Just over half the 15–24 age group were marmalade-eaters in 1985; by 1997 this figure had dropped to under 45 per cent. The former 15–24s, having now become the 25–34s, had not significantly increased their marmalade consumption as they set up homes and families of their own (in 1985 this sector had registered a steep rise in consumer numbers to nearly three-quarters of the age-group). By contrast, nearly 88 per cent of the over-65s were marmalade-eaters in 1985, and twelve years later the number of consumers in their age-group had suffered only a slight decline to just over 84 per cent.[10]

Only a few of the nationally known marmalade-making firms have been able to withstand on their own the commercial pressures of the late twentieth century. Of those mentioned here, Baxters of Speyside and Wilkin of Tiptree continue as independent family organisations, as does Duerr's, now the biggest such family firm. Most other companies of substantial size have been taken over as subsidiaries by large food conglomerates.

Today James Robertson is part of RHM (Rank Hovis McDougall) Foods; and the firm itself acquired the preserves section of Keiller in 1988. Robertson's is still our largest marmalade manufacturer. Frank Cooper has been absorbed by CPC and their distributors, Bestfoods Ltd; 'Oxford' survives as a trade name for the marmalade, which is no longer made in that city. Elsenham is owned by Cheergrey, who bought the company in December 1995. L. Rose and Company was acquired in 1957, and William P. Hartley and William Moorhouse and Sons in 1959, by Schweppes, who also bought the Chivers factory and farms in 1959 (the family bought back the farms two years later). Today Chivers Hartley is owned by Hillsdown Holdings, and marmalade and other preserves sold under the Chivers, Hartley, Moorhouse and Rose's brand names are all manufactured at the expanded Chivers factory at Histon.

The fortunes of James Keiller and Son, our oldest commercial manufacturer, have fluctuated during the twentieth century. By 1922, the family connection had been lost, and Keiller was completely controlled by Crosse & Blackwell, although the range of marmalades and the Dundee cakes and confectionery for which the firm had become famous continued to be marketed as before. After their London factory was destroyed by enemy action in the 1939–45 war, marmalade production was centred at Dundee where a second factory complex had been established at Maryfield. Keiller's marmalade enjoyed a boom in the 1950s, both in Britain and abroad. In the 1960s, when Nestlé had taken over the company, there was some decline; but in the course of the 1970s, sales of orange marmalade doubled, and the new grapefruit, lemon and three-fruits marmalades met with success. That was to prove the firm's undoing. In 1979, in anticipation of an expanding market, a costly extension was built at Maryfield and new plant installed there to create 'the first marmalade factory in the world to be controlled by microprocessors.' By the time it was ready, a world recession had seriously affected the export trade, and demand at home was falling.

During the 1980s the Keiller company was owned by a series of different firms until in 1988 its marmalade production was taken over by James Robertson & Sons of Manchester. Today the Keiller name survives attached to a 'Seville Orange Dundee' and to a new Roughcut Orange and Lemon marmalade, both relaunched in 1997. But despite the historic Dundee name, the marmalades themselves are produced at Robertson's Droylsden factory.

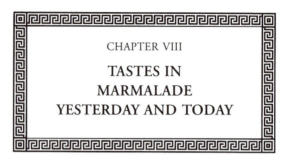

CHAPTER VIII

TASTES IN MARMALADE YESTERDAY AND TODAY

QUINCE MARMALADE AND OTHER NON-CITRUS MARMALADES

Marmalade, 'as is well known, is made from the Seville or bitter orange.'[1] So wrote Arthur Hassall in the 1850s, proving that orange marmalade had by then become the norm for most people and had ousted quince marmalade as the best known and most regularly eaten form of the preserve. Yet some people still fought a rearguard action on behalf of quince marmalade. A dozen years later, Anne Bowman's *The New Cookery Book* claimed, 'The most approved marmalades are orange and quince, the welcome addition to English and Scotch breakfast tables.'

But by then quince marmalade was in decline, and its consumption continued to wane. It remained in use mainly among those country-dwellers in southern Britain with access to quince trees, and those purchasers of marmalade who were prepared to meet the extra cost of what had become a special taste. For the growing populations of the industrial towns orange marmalade was the obvious choice, for quinces were not available to townspeople on any great scale, whereas Seville oranges arrived each year at the ports and were distributed countrywide by the railways.

The manufacturing firms produced quince marmalade on a small scale, compared with their orange marmalade output. It appears on a Crosse & Blackwell price-list of 1884, where it is offered in jars of a single, unidentified size, probably 1 lb. (450 gm.), whereas orange marmalade was to be had in either 1, 2, 3, 4, 7, or 14 lb. jars, and cost from 3 $^1/_2$ d. to 4 $^1/_2$ d. (1 $^1/_2$–2 p) a pound, compared with a possible 9d. (4 p) a pound for quince marmalade. Eventually the quince version was dropped by those firms which specialised in citrus marmalades, and quince preserves are now made mainly by those manufacturers who also produce jams and conserves from other less common fruits and berries.

During the twentieth century relatively few people have grown their own quinces and turned them into home-made marmalades. But recently there has been a surge of interest in preparing conserves from japonica quinces. The japonicas are related to the true quince, and they are to be found in British gardens today, grown for the sake of their red, orange or pink flowers, far more often than the more delicate true quince tree, *Cydonia vulgaris.*

Many nineteenth- and twentieth-century cookery-books give recipes for other non-citrus fruit marmalades, though the distinction between such marmalades and jam is not very easy to make. Some of them, like the ubiquitous apricot marmalade, had their origins in the days before the word 'jam' was coined. It is interesting that apricot marmalade, like quince and orange marmalades, had medicinal overtones. Jane Austen mentioned it in *Sense and Sensibility* as a balm for outward injuries; it 'had been successfully applied for a bruised temple' to the small, spoilt daughter of Sir John and Lady Middleton (in the context it may well have been applied internally as well as externally, but Miss Austen leaves that question to the reader's imagination).

Mrs Beeton has an apricot marmalade recipe (her other two marmalade fruits are quince and orange); and Crosse & Blackwell had apricot and peach marmalades as well as apricot and peach jams on their 1884 price-list. Today the distinction between the soft-fruit marmalades and jams of the same fruits is virtually lost, and in any census of taste such marmalades would be treated as jams.

TASTES IN ORANGE AND OTHER CITRUS FRUIT MARMALADES

Today the first marmalade question in many households is: coarse-cut chunky or jelly? Children often prefer jelly and sometimes insist on removing any fine-cut peel that reaches their toast or bread. Chivers' research on the subject revealed a distinct adult consumer preference in the matter. More older and male marmalade-eaters prefer the marmalades with thick-cut peel; more younger and female ones prefer the 'fine-cuts'. The view that a preference for coarse-cut marmalade is particularly male is borne out by the style of Frank Cooper's Oxford marmalade, with its exceptionally large, wide, flavourful pieces of orange peel, for its initial success was in the very masculine arena of the late nineteenth-century university among the dons and undergraduates; and since then it has been the choice of explorers – taken by Scott to the Antarctic and by Hillary to the heights of Everest. Nevertheless, recent research by Robertson's has shown that their traditional Golden Shred and Silver Shred marmalades nowadays have their greatest appeal among the over-45s of both sexes, though Golden Shred is still the largest-selling brand in the marmalade market.

The recognition of two distinct types of marmalade, allowing for a preference one way or the other, can be traced back to its earliest days. The quince version could be made either with all the pulp of the fruit, when it became opaque from the fruit-solids, or by filtering the juice after the first boiling and reboiling with sugar to yield a clear jelly (often referred to as quidony or quince jelly, not as marmalade at all). The orange and pippin marmalades of the seventeenth century were also made with an equivalent variation in technique. In some recipes apple and orange pulp were included in the finished product; in others, the apples were boiled in a little water and their juice was then strained out for jelly, to which was added orange peel, either beaten or cut into long, fine strips.

By the mid-eighteenth century, when apples had been dropped from most recipes, the choice lay between beaten or smooth marmalade, for which the orange-peel was boiled soft and pounded up to be set with the juice into an unclear jelly; and that which was made with shredded or 'chipped' peel, in England called transparent marmalade and in Scotland chip marmalade. The pounded, smooth marmalade corresponded to today's jelly marmalade, and the transparent to our marmalades with medium- or coarse-cut peel. Beaten marmalade is no longer made; but variant forms have continued, and the spectrum of variation has expanded to include numerous gradations of peel, from the very fine-cut to that in large and long pieces; as well as those marmalades in the form of a clear, totally peel-less jelly.

Another aspect of taste concerns the sweetness of marmalade. The earliest orange marmalades, made with pippins, contained at least as much sugar as fruit pulp, and they were almost certainly boiled for far too long by modern standards. Sometimes extra sugar was beaten into the cooked marmalade just before it cooled, which helped it to set as a solid paste, although some of the sugar must have recrystallised almost at once. But sugar was much loved during the seventeenth century and much used, even in places where we would not look for it today, for instance scattered over the lids of savoury pies or mixed with spinach, spices, and rosewater in tarts.

Conversely, the bitterness of Seville oranges was not appreciated, and the early orange marmalade recipes have the oranges soaked, boiled, and reboiled in several changes of water over a number of days, to try to remove some of that bitterness. In the eighteenth century when the skins of the bitter oranges were grated before marmalade-making began, again to take off some of the distinctive sour tang produced by the oils in the surface-layer of the peel, only a part of the 'grate' was added in again later, and sometimes none at all. Was the result simply sweet and insipid? Not necessarily, for orange marmalade at that time still had very little water added to it during its preparation. Moreover, it was made to be eaten as a dessert dish, not spread upon toast, or mixed with any other bland foodstuff. So the stronger flavour which we find acceptable could have seemed too intense, even overpowering, when the concentrated marmalade was consumed on its own.

During the nineteenth century, the jelly element in marmalade gradually developed a less solid consistency, owing to the extraction of extra pectin from the pips and the addition of more water to pulp and peel. The sweetness of the conserve was a little diminished, but not too much so. Finished home-made marmalade has to incorporate well over 65 per cent sugar if it is not to ferment or attract moulds while being stored.

More recently, Ministry of Food regulations have ensured that all marmalade manufactured for sale contained 68.5 per cent sugar (65 per cent if hermetically sealed). We have therefore become accustomed to marmalade of approximately that degree of sweetness. Some marmalades can taste sweeter than others, depending on the type and quantity of fruit pulp and peel in them. Wilkin of Tiptree, who have never used any chemical preservatives in their conserves, import whole frozen Seville oranges rather than the frozen pulp used by some other firms, so they can extract the fullest flavour from the fruit to counteract the inevitable sweetness of marmalades preserved only by their high sugar content.

During the past 25 years we have become more health-conscious, and more aware that high sugar consumption leads to obesity and increases the risk of developing the diseases of the affluent society. In 1977 Chivers identified a move away from 'sweet sticky' marmalades in consumer preference, and they introduced their Tangy Orange and Lemon Shred marmalades to meet it. The EEC regulations of 1981 permit the use of certain preservatives which allow jams and marmalades to be made with much less sugar, i.e. 48 per cent instead of the earlier 68.5 per cent. Several firms then introduced reduced-sugar marmalades and also increased their fruit to make 'extra' marmalades with an intensified fruit flavour to mask the added preservative. The 'extra' on the jar-label refers to the fruit content, as defined by another EEC regulation.

But Whole Earth created an orange marmalade sweetened only by apple juice and set with lime pectin (it required over 3 lb. of apples and oranges to make one twelve-ounce jarful). This type of marmalade will keep good for 18 months while still hermetically sealed, but once the seal is broken it must be stored in the refrigerator.

At present, Streamline market a diced-cut orange marmalade, protected by preservative, with the sugar reduced to 48 per cent and the fruit increased to 45 per cent, which is made in Denmark. Baxters produce an extra-fruit, reduced-sugar, three-fruits marmalade which retails for less than their full-sugar, luxury 'orange, lemon and grapefruit' variety. But Whole Earth have progressed into fruit spreads. These fruit spreads based on marmalade fruits are a development which in some respects echoes the eighteenth-century concept of beaten marmalade.

Stute currently offer a 'fine cut diabetic orange extra marmalade'. It is sweetened with sorbitol, but does not contain preservatives, and therefore needs to be refrigerated once the jar has been opened. But diabetic marmalade may soon be a thing of the past. Boots the Chemist, who were the first to introduce it, have now withdrawn all their former 'diabetic' products sweetened with sorbitol. Thinking about diet for the diabetes sufferer has changed, and such people are now encouraged to plan their own diets, eating a normal range of foods but including only small, controlled amounts of sugar-rich foodstuffs. In this context, reduced-sugar marmalades are likely to become a practical replacement for the former 'diabetic' versions.

A fairly recent innovation, made in response to the latest campaign for healthy eating, is 'organic' marmalade manufactured from organically grown fruit and sugar. Hartley produce an organic thin-cut orange marmalade, and Wilkin's range includes a medium-cut organic orange marmalade, with a high fruit content and reduced sugar. Initial sales have been promising. Duerr's 'conservation grade' marmalade is also made from organically grown oranges. The market for this type of preserve, currently still fairly small, is likely to increase as more consumers insist on buying organically grown fresh fruit and vegetables.

Taste is an elusive quality. The majority of marmalade purchasers still prefer traditional sweet marmalades; but some people now prefer the less sweet 'extra' fruit marmalades, while others are partial to the newer marmalades made of citrus fruits other than Seville oranges. The best selling of all Wilkin's jams and marmalades, surpassing even their famous strawberry conserves, is reported to be their tangerine and orange Double One marmalade.

Marmalades come with a big price differential, and those at the quality end of the market can cost at least twice as much as supermarket own-label ones. The consumer's choice will therefore be influenced by disposable income as well as personal flavour preferences. For some people, home-made marmalade is the chosen alternative, although it is only an economical one if the maker's time and labour is not costed in. Those in a hurry can still buy the canned Seville orange or lemon pulp prepared by Mamade, and turn out an everyday marmalade from it.

Regional differences in marmalade consumption have changed since 1981. By 1997 just over 78 per cent of the people of South West England were marmalade consumers, the highest regional percentage in Britain. Second to them came the inhabitants of South East England and East Anglia, with over 73.5 per cent. Yorkshire and Humberside, home to more consumers than any other region in 1981, had dropped in the interim to seventh place on the list, with just under 66 per cent of marmalade-eaters; while Scotland, ninth and last on the list, had below 64.5 per cent of them.[2]

The changes in the consumption pattern reflect changes in breakfasting habits. More people than before breakfast solely on cereals and milk, along with tea or coffee; and some younger people have abandoned the formal meal altogether, and begin their day with snack foods of various kinds. Ethnic minority groups tend to retain their own food preferences over several generations, and are unlikely to adopt the British toast and marmalade as breakfast fare. Nevertheless, marmalade continues to be enjoyed by the majority of people in Britain.

MARMALADE AS A HEALTH FOOD

Marmalade, though not in the forefront of health foods, does carry some health-enhancing qualities. A part of the vitamin C is retained in the pulp and peel, even after cooking. Another ingredient of the pulp and the white inner peel of citrus fruits is the group of substances known as bioflavinoids, which both reduce the need for vitamin C and make that which is present more effective, thus speeding up the healing process for injuries of every type.[3]

Again, the appetite-enhancing property of marmalade has never been forgotten. In the words of *Cassell's Domestic Dictionary*, c.1884, 'It is exceedingly wholesome, and the slight bitterness which belongs to orange marmalade helps to stimulate the appetite of those who require a relish with their food.' Frank Cooper elaborated on this theme in an advertisement for Oxford marmalade in the *Oxford Review* of 20 October 1913, which claimed, 'It is a tonic; it aids digestion; it cleanses the palate.' And in 1945 Chivers were still recommending their Olde English marmalade on their price-list as prepared 'by a special process which preserves the tonic properties and bitter appetising flavour of the fruit.'

Today's health-giving marmalades fall into two categories, and those whose taste in marmalade is linked to their quest for health-promoting foodstuffs will have to make their choice accordingly. People who believe that sugar is the enemy of fitness will select the marmalades containing much less sugar, but with added preservatives. In these, there is no danger that the sweetness will overwhelm the fruit flavour, as formerly tended to happen with marmalades of the 'sweet, sticky' variety. The sugar-reduced marmalades will appeal particularly to those who have become so accustomed to lower levels of sugar elsewhere in their diet that they find sweet marmalades too cloying.

People who prefer to eat a totally natural product containing no artificial preservatives will tend towards the traditional pure fruit and sugar marmalades, whether home-made or commercially produced, and if they wish to counter the inevitable sweetness of conserves containing a high proportion of sugar they will have to spread them more thinly, or alternate toast and marmalade with plain toast and a little butter. Whichever way the consumers react, the manufacturers will study their preferences carefully and will be ready, as they have been for so many years past, to create new recipes to point up particular characteristics of the citrus fruits, or combine them in fresh ways, in order to win more customers for their own specially-developed marmalades.

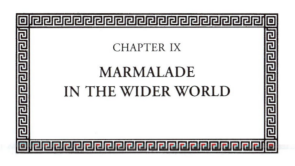

CHAPTER IX

MARMALADE
IN THE WIDER WORLD

MARMALADE IN THE NEW WORLD: THE EARLY CENTURIES

Marmalade travelled with European settlers to many new-found lands from the sixteenth century onwards. It is unlikely that it was actually carried there, except in very small amounts. But the colonists took with them the seeds of the necessary fruit-bearing trees; and also the recipes of the home country, sometimes in printed books but more usually in the manuscript household books on which emigrant housewives depended not only for instructions on cookery and preserving, but also for medical remedies in time of sickness.

The citrus fruits appear to have crossed the Atlantic earlier than quinces, for Christopher Columbus took the seeds of oranges, lemons, and citrons with him on his second voyage to the West Indies in 1493. They grew readily there, and the trees were abundantly fruitful. It is less certain when quinces were introduced into the Portuguese and Spanish New World colonies but they must have arrived soon afterwards. Thus there is every likelihood that quince marmalade made after the fashion of southern Europe was consumed in some of those Portuguese and Spanish colonies during the sixteenth century, not only on the islands, but also on the South American mainland. Eventually such marmalade came to be produced on a commercial basis. A famous manufactory of quince marmalade existed in Cuba during the nineteenth century, for the conserve was then still appreciated as a health food by North Americans, who favoured Cuba as a place for convalescence and recuperation through the period 1800–1870.[1]

The citrus fruits too were conserved with sugar. Friar Joseph de Acosta, a visitor to the Indies, returned to Spain to publish his account of the islands in 1590. In it he wrote that, of all the fruits introduced into them, the orange was 'the one that has most widely spread in the Indies, because I have not seen a single region where there were no oranges… The preserves of candied oranges which they make in the Indies are the best that I have tasted anywhere.'[2] The orange conserves may well have taken the form of the beaten orange and sugar pastes of contemporary recipe-books. If so, they may have lacked the rosewater which went into the European versions, and have tasted all the better without it. There is another possibility. Sweet oranges had been planted in the islands, as well as the bitter Seville types, and the sweet orange fruits may have been conserved. If so, that would indicate an early example of the preference of southern Europeans for sweet orange 'marmalade' which they still retain today.

Citrus fruits were first brought to the North American mainland in the mid-sixteenth century, when small Spanish settlements survived for a time in Florida. Florida remained Spanish until 1763, but only after 1822 did white American settlers from further north arrive in any considerable numbers and they found that bitter-orange trees had naturalised themselves in profusion there, along with some sweet-orange trees.

At the time when the earliest English settlers reached North America, they made their landfall much further north, and of course knew nothing of the Florida oranges. They brought with them the seeds of English fruit trees, including quinces, and the first marmalades of North America were therefore made from the original marmalade fruit, the quince. Quince trees, and other fruit trees of British origin, quickly established themselves. After his second voyage to New England in 1663, John Josselyn was able to report, 'The quinces, cherries, damsons, set the dames on work, marmelad and preserved damson is to be met with in every house.'[3]

Contemporary English recipes were used to make the quinces into marmalade. Some examples may be seen in *Martha Washington's Booke of Cookery and Booke of Sweetmeats* (a seventeenth-century manuscript which later came into the hands of Martha Washington of Virginia). Here six recipes for preserving quinces, red, yellow or white, are followed by seven for quince marmalade, red, white or 'ordinary'. Other seventeenth-century family manuscripts from Pennsylvania and Connecticut contain similar recipe collections, both for cookery and preserving, showing that the settlers in their early years clung to the cuisine of Britain and were slow to exploit the indigenous plant-foods of North America.[4]

Although the Florida orange-groves remained unknown to the Americans of New England, there was some trade in the oranges and lemons of the West Indies and hence the possibility of making orange marmalades and preserves. As in the case of quince marmalade, the recipes for these had originated in England. *Martha Washington's Booke of Sweetmeats* includes just one for orange marmalade, a typical seventeenth-century recipe using cooked, pounded orange-peel, the pulp of pippins, and sugar wetted with rosewater. A pippin jelly also appears there, which has sliced candied orange-peels and orange- and lemon-juice added to the apple-juice; and this is comparable to the pippin jellies of Restoration England.[5] [See R 12.] In the same American book are recipes for quidonies made from the juices of several different fruits jellied with sugar, and printed in moulds; and there is a 'marmalet' of mulberries or raspberries.

North American cookery continued to develop under strong English influence through the eighteenth century. The printed cookery-books then available were still the English ones (Hannah Glasse's *The Art of Cookery* was especially popular) and it was the end of the century before they even began to be supplemented by books compiled by native-born Americans. During those years, in North America as in England, the older, stiff, dry slicing-marmalade was gradually superseded by the thick, sticky, but no longer dry conserve, put up in glasses and sealed with brandy-papers. It was eaten as a dessert dish, and it also retained its medicinal function, to strengthen and comfort the stomach and to stimulate the appetite. Nevertheless, slicing-marmalade was still made occasionally at an even later date. There is a recipe for a beaten marmalade made from the peels of lemons which have been used for lemonade in *Domestic Cookery* by Elizabeth Ellicott Lea, first published in 1845, which concludes: 'When cold, cut it in slices for the table; it will keep several weeks.' [See R 19.]

Early in the nineteenth century, the marmalade of England began to change its role, under Scottish influence, from dessert dish to breakfast spread. In that role, Seville orange marmalade was at first supreme, and it was the marmalade destined to travel to all those countries to which British settlers thenceforth carried their food customs.

The North American states, by contrast, had already freed themselves from British dominion. The British food tradition was still influential there but, in several aspects, it was the influences of the previous two centuries which continued to be felt; and this is apparent in attitudes to marmalade. In the first place, the word 'marmalade' remained in use in North America for conserves of non-citrus fruits to a greater extent than in England, where the term 'jam' gradually ousted it. That term had been coined in the second half of the seventeenth century, when the first North American settlers were already well established in their new homes. So when the word 'jam' eventually followed them across the Atlantic, it did not obtain quite the same currency among them as

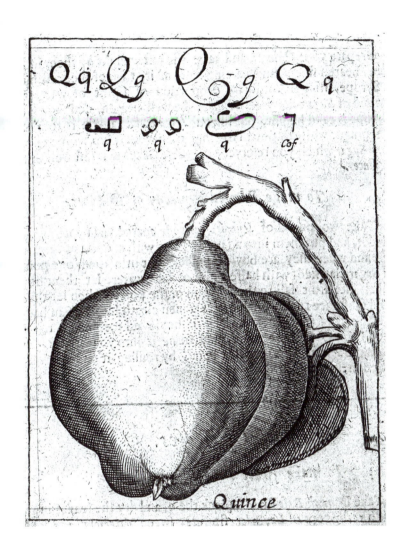

17th-century quince. *A Book of Fruits & Flowers*, 1653.

it did in England, even during the nineteenth century. The American cookbooks of that period contain many recipes for marmalades of apples, pears, peaches, grapes, cherries, greengages, pineapples, and other non-citrus fruits, as well as the long-established quince marmalade.

Another result of North America's early acquaintance with marmalade was that it had entered the country as a dessert dish. During the nineteenth century, when ties with Britain were no longer as close, it did not develop into a breakfast spread in the American states to the same extent as it did in Britain. Fannie Farmer's eighteen different breakfast menus in *The Boston Cooking-School Cook Book*, 1899, do not give a mention to marmalade, though one menu includes buckwheat cakes with maple-syrup, an indication that North Americans welcomed very sweet spreads or sauces at breakfast time.

Fifty years earlier, Elizabeth Ellicott Lea described her cider marmalade, made with apples, cider and sugar, as 'a pleasant sauce for dinner, or eaten with bread and butter at tea'. Similar usages could be found for the citrus-fruit marmalades, for the bitterness of Seville oranges and the sharp flavour of lemons gave them some appeal in the role of sweet pickles to accompany meat. This was especially true of the lemon and tomato marmalades devised in North America, appropriately since the tomato was native to the New World. According to a modern recipe, such marmalade has usually been served with a meat course at tea or supper and is 'always a prime favourite with the menfolk'. The same tradition could explain why, in recent years, American students studying at colleges in England have been known to eat their breakfast marmalade with their fried bacon, as a relish.

During the nineteenth century, orange marmalade in North America was still made with Seville or bittersweet oranges. The bitter-orange trees of the Florida groves were then producing their natural fruits (they have since become rootstocks for sweet-orange and other citrus-fruit trees); and the West Indian islands were also a source of supply. Through most of the century Seville oranges from Cuba were imported into Pennsylvania for marmalade-making.[6] Fannie Farmer recommended sour, smooth-skinned (i.e. bittersweet) oranges for the purpose, 'and allow three-fourths their weight in sugar'. The peels of oranges of this variety boil clear when made into marmalade, but their sweet juice and pulp do not have the characteristic Seville-orange flavour; and their use no doubt paved the way towards the sweet orange marmalade which was to become more usual in the twentieth century.

Fannie Farmer also gave instructions for making orange and rhubarb marmalade (8 bittersweet oranges to 5 lb. rhubarb), probably developed under the influence of Mrs Beeton's 'Rhubarb and orange jam to resemble Scotch marmalade'. But several of the North American nineteenth-century cookbooks offer only non-citrus marmalades, suggesting that in some states the trade in Seville and bittersweet oranges was small, or hardly existed.

Further north, in the Canadian provinces, British food traditions became dominant among the English-speaking population after 1761. Scottish settlers ensured that orange marmalade arrived as a breakfast food and that it was the Seville orange marmalade familiar in Britain. The oranges had to be imported from much further south and before the end of the nineteenth century ready-made marmalade was also being sent from Britain to Canada by the marmalade manufacturers.

In the West Indian islands, the earliest New World home of the citrus trees, their fruits continued to flourish and to support the local economy, since they were shipped to North America and to Europe. In the islands which were colonies of Britain orange marmalade was made and eaten in the British manner. But marmalade-making was not limited to Seville oranges. Not only bitter and sweet oranges, but also lemons, limes, citrons, pomelos, and eventually grapefruits and tangerines, were raised, so the inhabitants of the islands were able to produce conserves very easily from any of these fruits combined with locally-produced sugar. It was probably the discovery that lime and grapefruit and tangerine marmalades were already being made in the West Indies which encouraged British marmalade manufacturers to introduce these exotic citrus marmalades into Britain late in the nineteenth century.[7]

MARMALADE IN BRITISH COLONIAL LIFE: THE NINETEENTH CENTURY

British cuisine was to follow the flag to other parts of the world during the nineteenth century. That cuisine included the production of Britain's Seville orange marmalade and its consumption at the breakfast table; and from the point of view of the settlers' marmalade supplies, it was convenient that so many of Britain's recently-acquired territories lay in tropical or semi-tropical zones which permitted the cultivation of citrus fruits.

The fruits had grown since time immemorial in India, and from India they reached eastern Africa at an early and unknown date. Their arrival in southern Africa is more specifically chronicled. Oranges were introduced at the Cape by the Dutch in 1654, and lemons and limes soon afterwards.[8] The British settlers who took their marmalade recipes to South Africa found the fruits they needed growing locally; and they continued to make and to consume marmalade in the same manner as the Britons of the home country. Late in the nineteenth century, Hildagonda Duckitt, a Cape housekeeper for many years, published a compendium of her favourite recipes, among them a number of typical south African dishes displaying Dutch influence. But her two marmalade recipes are for marmalade in the British style, published under the names of the two English ladies who supplied them (one is, however, for 'Marmalade (Scotch)'; it begins with the oranges gently boiled whole for two hours and it mentions, a propos of cutting them up, that 'some people mince everything through a mincing machine').

India was the very early home of the citrus fruits, whence they reached Persia and were there discovered by the Arabs who spread them into the Mediterranean lands. During the second half of the nineteenth century several household books were published in London to advise the British families of the Raj on culinary and domestic matters in their new homes. Recipes in some of these books suggest that marmalade was made with either sweet oranges, sour oranges, or lemons, whichever were available in the markets at the time; and the Indian weights by which they were sold were also explained. [See R 20.]

The first Australian settlers had purchased supplies at the Cape in 1787. These included oranges, lemons, sugar-canes, vines, and quinces; and early in the following year they set their seeds not far from Sydney Cove. The Rev. Richard Johnson reported that his orange-trees had reached two feet high by August 1790 and were 'very promising'. Within a few years there were groves of oranges and other citrus fruits along the Parramatta river; and in 1839 a visitor, Louisa Anne Meredith, observed among their fruits a new type of lemon and 'a pretty fragrant fruit called a mandarin orange'.[9]

Orange and lemon marmalades were made according to recipes brought out from Britain. From the mid-1860s Australian cookery-books began to be published and these show that the type of marmalade favoured until the turn of the century was still the old, dense, sticky marmalade. There is even a 'grated marmalade', in J. Pearson's *Australian Cookery: Recipes for the People,* made with the gratings of the orange-peel, the sieved pulp, and only a gill ($^1/_4$ pint) of water to 20 bitter oranges and a lemon, which hardly differs from the beaten marmalades of the eighteenth and early nineteenth-century English cookery-books. [See R 21.]

Citrus fruits were also introduced in due course in the North Island of New Zealand. The New Zealand settlers' diet was very limited in the early years. But they aimed to follow British food traditions. So they raised bitter-orange trees as well as sweet ones, and were able to make bitter-orange marmalades on the pattern of those made in Britain and to follow British practice in eating them as breakfast spreads.

While the home marmalade-makers were active in all the countries mentioned, and in several others where British expatriates tried to re-create their former way of life, supplies of the conserve were also sent out to them. Scottish marmalade was being made 'in large quantities for exportation ... and potted in large jars' in the 1800s, according to Margaret Dods. Exportation at first meant a voyage to London or other ports of southern England and before long to Welsh and Irish ports too, because at the time shipboard provided the easiest and most economical method of transporting goods in bulk. But it also demonstrated that marmalade travelled well by sea.

Ireland followed Great Britain in the field of marmalade-making and consumption, but the conserve was neither made nor eaten there as universally as in Britain. Away from the big ports, transport problems influenced the availability – and the cost – both of Seville oranges and of imported ready-made marmalade so that during the nineteenth century marmalade remained something of a luxury food.

But its exportation from Scotland soon became a more ambitious business. Marmalade was sent across the Atlantic to Canada and the American states. Even Australia was not too far. William Kelly, who visited Melbourne in 1853 at the time of the gold rush, reported on the international range of foodstuffs obtainable close to the diggings, including 'the ham of York, the marmalade of Scotland, the sardines of France, the condiments of India ... only waiting a beckon to jump down our throats from the surrounding shelves.'[10]

The preserve was little affected by extremes of temperature on the voyage and, indeed, long journeys and long keeping could actually improve it. So it was sent out, not only to expatriate

Britons but to others who had discovered that British marmalade was a special delicacy. Wilkin of Tiptree still keep records of distinguished customers abroad to whom they despatched jams and marmalades at the turn of the century; among them were the Empress of Russia and the Queen of Greece (both grand-daughters of Queen Victoria, which may explain their predilection), and the Queen of Spain.

Individual travellers too, and even explorers, carried English or Scottish marmalade with them in their personal baggage, partly out of nostalgia and partly because of the continuing belief in its tonic properties. Today Frank Cooper can show, as their most prized possession, a tin of their marmalade which was taken to the Antarctic on Captain Scott's expedition of 1911–12 and was recovered, still in perfect condition, by the expedition which retraced his route in 1980.

MARMALADE IN THE WIDER WORLD TODAY

It is time to take a brief look at the marmalade situation today in some of the countries where its earlier history has been recounted. The most noteworthy fact to emerge from such a survey is that citrus fruit marmalades are to be met with in all of them, but the position of Seville orange marmalade as the principal form has been eroded.[11]

In the United States it was already losing ground to other conserves during the nineteenth century, and several recipe-books ignored it, giving instructions only for the making of marmalades of non-citrus fruits. When orange marmalade is made there now, it is most often based upon sweet oranges, and modern editions of Fannie Farmer's famous cookbook no longer recommend the 'sour smooth-skinned' oranges of the nineteenth-century recipe. The remaining wild orange groves of Florida provide stocks for sweet oranges or other citrus fruits, and huge numbers of sweet oranges are grown in the state. California is also a major producer of sweet oranges and they are raised on a smaller scale in Louisiana, Arizona, and Texas. Travellers breakfasting in hotels and restaurants and aboard aircraft are offered sweet orange marmalade, but only as a poor third to grape jelly and strawberry jam, the preferred breakfast preserves in North America today.

To plot in detail the pattern of marmalade-making and consumption in the United States over the past fifty years would be an enormous task; and here it is only possible to cast a brief, impressionistic glance over it. A few enthusiasts still make their own marmalade, nowadays often from limes or lemons. But cans of prepared Seville orange peel and pulp are occasionally to be seen on supermarket shelves, as proof that such marmalade is not totally ignored. In the southern states, golden jellies are still produced from lemons or from combinations of sweet oranges, grapefruits, and limes, and these are forms of jelly marmalade.

The imported English and Scottish marmalades also have a role, often as a small food-gift. Although these marmalades are widely purchased, they tend not to go into everyday use, but to sit for long periods on the refrigerator shelf before a suitable occasion can be found to broach them. It is probably true to say that interest in Seville orange marmalade, apart from the contents of the imported jars which perhaps achieve some distinction as an ethnic foodstuff, is now at a low ebb.

In Canada, by contrast, marmalade usage remains very close to that of Britain. During recent years there has been some decline in consumption because of changes in breakfast habits – again as in Britain. But each year, during the few weeks of their season, the imported Seville oranges appear on sale, ready for the use of the home marmalade-makers. For those who prefer to purchase it ready-made there are plentiful supplies of bitter orange marmalade manufactured in Canada, while imported marmalades from Britain can always be found at any good grocery-store or supermarket, and from time to time marmalade from other countries too, such as

Spain and Australia. The imported British marmalades include the well-known lemon, lime, and ginger varieties. Nowadays it is the older generation who are most partial to Seville orange marmalade; younger people with a sweet tooth find its tanginess too bitter. But there is still a strong predilection among Canadians for Seville orange marmalade, eaten at breakfast with buttered toast or 'English muffins'.

The breakfast marmalade tradition of the British Isles has also held strong much further south, in those West Indian islands which were under British rule before they achieved independence. In many of them citrus fruits are still an economic crop, and the trees also grow readily in gardens as they have done for nearly five hundred years. Marmalade is frequently home-made, though not always from Seville oranges, for people simply prepare it from the fruits on their garden trees, which may be bitter or sweet oranges, lemons, limes, grapefruits, mandarins, or from a mixture of the fruits available. It was perhaps the readiness of the West Indians to mix their marmalade fruits which led Rose's, in England, to give their thick-cut orange, grapefruit and lime preserve the name 'West Indian marmalade' when they launched it in the 1950s.[12] The availability of such a variety of citrus fruits has also led to the creation of some delicious local marmalades, such as the one made of fresh green-skinned tangerines served at the Montpellier Plantation Inn on Nevis, one of the Leeward Islands, and described by a visitor in the 1980s as 'the world's best marmalade'.[13]

In southern and eastern Africa, expatriate Britons can make their own marmalades from citrus fruits grown in the low-lying areas. The fruits are, of course, transported to those regions where the climate does not favour citrus trees. But marmalade-making in the heights can lead to problems. At over six thousand feet, the sugar boils too quickly and may not invert successfully, thus yielding a marmalade that can ferment and become highly alcoholic within a short time. Marmalades imported from Britain can usually be bought, and in southern Africa local brands too, such as the 'All Gold' sold in Lesotho and Botswana. And canned, prepared citrus fruit pulp is available here, as in other parts of the world, for those who wish to make marmalade quickly and easily.

The black Africans have not adopted marmalade or other preserves to any great extent because the wheat bread to accompany them is not a regular part of their diet. When they do choose to eat marmalade – and wheat bread – they tend to purchase the imported marmalades.

Australia and New Zealand for a long time followed Britain in the practice of spreading Seville orange marmalade on breakfast bread or toast. In Australia, although the orange and lemon groves bordering the Parramatta river have disappeared, citrus trees are raised elsewhere in New South Wales, and on a considerable scale in Victoria. New Zealand's citrus fruits are produced on the North Island, and in the last few decades grapefruits have become the most popular variety. It is perhaps because both countries are able to grow their own marmalade fruits and thus to concentrate on those types which prove to be best-liked on the home market that they have been more ready to move away from the traditional Seville orange marmalade of Britain's breakfast.

A Victoria Department of Agriculture bulletin of the 1930s shows that the lime, lemon, citronella (a small lime-shaped fruit of bright orange colour), and grapefruit were each then in use as marmalade fruits in Australia. The favourite bitter orange was the Poorman, a name originally belonging to a rough-skinned fruit, but later applied also to the bittersweet, smooth-skinned Flat Seville. But the 'jam oranges', as the various Seville oranges were called, had already begun to yield to sweet oranges in marmalade, the latter preferred by some people 'because of the mild flavour'.[14] And that was an indicator of the direction in which Australian marmalade was heading. Australians have a notoriously sweet tooth when it comes to food; even their beers are sweeter than those in Britain.

During the last few decades they have largely abandoned bitter orange marmalade and most of the locally-manufactured marmalade today is made from sweet oranges.

Home-makers of marmalade who find the sweet oranges insipid temper them with lemons or grapefruits. In any case, they do not confine themselves to sweet oranges but turn readily to other citrus fruits – mandarins, cumquats, grapefruits, or any other variety in seasonal heavy supply at the local market, or growing abundantly on a tree in the garden at home. Seville oranges reach just a few market-stalls in Melbourne and Sydney in their season, but the numbers are not great.

Manufactured bitter orange marmalade can still be bought in the cities (a favourite brand is Lackersteen's Seville orange marmalade from Victoria), but it is much more difficult to find in the shops than the ubiquitous sweet orange marmalade. The Australian marmalade market has been an expanding one through the 1990s, with Cottee's manufacturing over half of the total amount sold, much of it under their own label. But a proportion of their output is devoted to their premium Monbulk and Rose's marmalades (the latter sold under labels very similar to Rose's jar labels in Britain, for Cottee's, like Rose's, are part of the Cadbury Schweppes conglomerate). A wide range of marmalades exported to Australia from Britain is also on sale in delicatessens and on speciality food counters of supermarkets and stores, more expensive than local kinds, but bought from time to time for the sake of variety.

Australians tend to prefer chewy, chunky marmalades to jelly types. Although marmalade consumption has fallen in their part of the world over the long term, due, as elsewhere, to changing breakfast habits, it seems to be holding its own with the younger generation, in contrast to jam (said to have now become 'apparently almost a peasant food'[15]).

New Zealanders, like Australians, eat their breakfast marmalade spread on bread or toast. Formerly, in New Zealand as elsewhere,

Seville orange marmalade was the usual choice. The citrus fruit grown in the north of North Island included bitter oranges, and the Poorman orange, the predominant variety, was often named in the marmalade recipes of the cookery-books.

Today it is hardly grown. The favourite citrus fruit in New Zealand is now the grapefruit. Several varieties are raised, and the favourite bitter fruit marmalade has therefore become grapefruit marmalade. This is the kind made up and sold by local manufacturers, and for a sweeter alternative they modify the flavour of the grapefruits by adding sweet oranges; and sweeter-tasting marmalades are also made from tangelos, hybrid citrus fruits crossed from the tangerine and the grapefruit. Those who desire Seville orange marmalade must seek out the marmalades imported from Britain and sold at gourmet shops and the special food counters in large supermarkets.

Home marmalade-makers also tend to grapefruit, alone or mixed with sweet oranges, though lime marmalade and lemon marmalade are sometimes made. Fewer people nowadays carry out all the preparation themselves, preferring to make up the preserve from tinned pre-cooked grapefruit with added pectin (a well-known brand is Pool's 'Mix'n'Made'; and Pool's also make a sweet orange version); or, more recently, from packs of pre-cooked and frozen grapefruit. Thus New Zealanders who continue to prefer the slight bitterness formerly associated with Seville oranges for their marmalade achieve it today in combination with the flavour of their preferred fruit, the grapefruit.

In the smaller territories under British influence, marmalade imported from Britain is usually on sale, but home marmalade-makers are dependent on the availability and cheapness of the citrus fruits. Thus in Hong Kong, where there is no space to grow citrus trees, during the years of British rule marmalade-lovers bought imported brands in the shops (which, not surprisingly, had little appeal for the Chinese). In Fiji, where oranges and lemons grow and there is a special abundance of pineapples, the latter are combined with citrus fruits for home-made marmalades. But in most places in the world where people of British stock have settled in the last 150 years, they have enjoyed marmalade for breakfast, sometimes making it from different citrus fruits, sometimes using local dark sugars, but always producing a conserve that is in some way related to the original Seville orange marmalades; and if they are unable to make marmalade themselves, then in very many cases, British marmalade firms send out supplies to fill the gap.

Moreover, the trading endeavours of English and Scottish manufacturers have also introduced Britain's Seville orange marmalade to a number of non-British nations. A Chivers' price-list of February 1945 advertised their Olde English marmalade in three languages, English, French and Spanish, showing that trade with friendly European countries was already picking up, although the end of the

Chivers' price-list, February 1945.

1939–45 war in Europe was still three months off. Today some firms export marmalade to more than 40 countries, worldwide.

Marian McNeill, in the 1960s, wrote of French hostesses who greeted her with the words, 'Voulez-vous du Dundi?', offering the marmalade with pride.[16] It is interesting to note that the French, when they are not entertaining British visitors, are still inclined to eat their marmalade as *confiture* for dessert; and this practice extends to French colonial territories, too. A recent Australian visitor to the western Pacific island of New Caledonia (French since 1854) felt some surprise on being confronted with a plate of marmalade as a dessert. But this food custom, like the naturalised Seville orange trees growing on the island, is a French legacy, for despite its name (bestowed by Captain Cook), New Caledonia had no early Scottish settlers.

The British marmalade firms continue to seek new markets worldwide. Nevertheless it is still under a threat which has nothing to do with flavour or quality. Ian Thurgood of Wilkin & Sons reports that, although there has been little change in the legislation controlling marmalade over the past 15 years, 'our greatest concern without doubt has been the continuing efforts of some European Community member states to have the term "marmalade" dropped in favour of "orange jam". Fortunately they have not succeeded so far, but we do wonder if the days of traditional British marmalade are numbered, and another part of our identity will be lost.' The basic problem is that other Europeans do not share the British predilection for Seville orange and other citrus fruit marmalades. They have a single term – often 'marmelada' or something similar – for all their sweet fruit conserves, and they refuse to recognise the difference between marmalade and jam. They want a single word to translate their single term.

Seville orange marmalade has been part of Britain's culinary heritage for more than four centuries. We must continue the fight to preserve its name and identity in the new millennium.

REFERENCES

I. MARMALADE AND ITS FORERUNNERS

1. A. Keiller, *Windmill Hill and Avebury Excavations* (1965), 41.
2. Cato, *De Re Rustica,* 143; Apicius, *The Roman Cookery Book,* ed. B. Flower and E. Rosenbaum(1958), 1.12.1;6 and 3.
3. Columella, *De Re Rustica,* 12.57.1–4; Dioscorides, *De Materia Medica,* 5.21–22; Pliny, *Natural History,* 15.60; Martial, *Epigrams,* 7.25.7.
4. Palladius, *Opus Agriculturae,* 11.20.
5. Paul of Aegina, *De Re Medica,* 7. 11.28 and 30.
6. Columella, *De Re Rustica,* 12.10.3.
7. Isidore of Seville, *Etymologiae,* 17.7.5.
8. J. Corominas, *Diccionario Crítico Etimológico de la Lengua Castellana,* Berne (1954), under *Membrillo.*
9. Strabo, *Geographia,* 15.1.20; Pliny, *Natural History,* 12.17; Dioscorides, *De Materia Medica,* 2.82.4.
10. A. J. Arberry, 'A Baghdad Cookery Book', *Islamic Culture* 13 (1939), intro., 23, 27–9.
11. M. Rodinson, 'Recherches sur les Documents Arabes relatifs à la Cuisine', *Revue des Études Islamiques* 17 (1949), 131.
12. S. Battaglia, *Grande Dizionario della Lingua Italiana,* Turin (1975), under *Marmellata* (quoting Sassetti).
13. *Le Ménagier de Paris,* ed. G. E. Brereton and J. M. Ferrier, Oxford (1981), 269; E. Faccioli, *Arte della Cucina* (Milan, 1966), vol. 1, 104–5 (Liber per cuoco).
14. *Two Fifteenth Century Cookery Books,* ed. T. Austin (Early English Text Society) (1888), 106.
15. J. Russell, *Boke of Nurture,* ed. F. J. Furnivall (EETS) (1868), 5–6.
16. R. Warner, *Antiquitates Culinariae* (1791), 76.
17. E. Brunskill, 'A Mediaeval Book of Herbs and Medicine', *Northwestern Naturalist* N.S.1 (1953–54), 185.

18. T. Dawson, *The Good Huswifes Iewell...with additions* (1596), 33v.; 34v.; A.W., *A Book of Cookrye* (1587), 42v.; J. Gerard, *The Herball* (1597), 1264–5.
19. Alexis of Piedmont, *The Secrets of . . . Alexis of Piedmont* (1562), 62.

II. 'FOREIGN AND HOME-BRED MARMALADES': TUDOR AND STUART ENGLAND

1. A. Glasfurd, *The Anti-pope (Peter de Luna, 1342–1423)* (1963), 263, 272, n. 45.
2. I am indebted to Dr Wendy Childs, of the School of History, University of Leeds, for allowing me to use her transcripts of port records referring to early imports of marmalade. Marmalade was still a very new commodity for England at the end of the fifteenth century, and had not yet begun to be taxed at some other southern ports, such as Bristol. No records of marmalade brought in on Italian ships at such an early date have yet come to light.
3. N. S. B. Gras, *The Early English Customs System* (Cambridge, Mass., 1918), 700, 703.
4. *A Collection of Ordinances and Regulations for the Government of the Royal Household* (Society of Antiquaries) (1790), Ordinances for the household of George, Duke of Clarence.
5. *The Lisle Letters,* ed. M. St C. Byrne, 6 vols. (Chicago, 1981), No. 854b.
6. L. F. Salzman, *English Trade in the Middle Ages* (1931), 412.
7. *Report on the MSS of Lord Middleton preserved at Wollaton Hall* (Royal Historical Manuscripts Commission) (1911), 455.
8. *Oxford English Dictionary,* corrected reissue 1970, 13 vols., under *Marmalade.*
9. *Lisle letters,* Nos. 192, 799a.
10. Ibid., Nos. 586, 797a, 1023, 1620.
11. F. P. de La Varenne, *Le nouveau et scavant Cuisinier françois* (Paris, 1669), part 3, 42.
12. F. G. Emmison, *Tudor Secretary: Sir William Petre at Court and Home (1961), 171.*
13. S. Pepys, *Diary,* ed. R. Latham & W. Matthews, vol. 4 (1971), 361, 363.
14. Warner, *Antiq. Cul.,* 119.
15. Dudley accounts in: *Calendar of the MSS of the most Honourable the Marquis of Bath, 5: Talbot, Dudley and Devereux,* ed. G. D. Owen (Royal Historical Manuscripts Commission) (1980), 149.

16. J. J. Lambert, *Records of the Skinners of London* (1933), 203.
17. W. Harrison, *Elizabethan England,* ed. F. J. Furnivall and L. Withington (Scott Library) (1902), 92.
18. Examples of posy-mats can be seen at certain museums, e.g. the Museum of London.
19. Sir T. Elyot, *The Castel of Helth, corrected and . . . augmented* (1541), 25.
20. *Lisle letters,* No. 898.
21. Gerard,*Herball,* 1264.
22. W. Langham, *The Garden of Health* (2nd ed . 1633), 512.
23. Emmison, *Tudor Secretary,* 252.
24. *Oxford English Dictionary* under *Marmalade* gives references for the works cited in this and the previous paragraph.
25. J. Josselyn, *An Account of Two Voyages to New England* (1674), 162.
26. *Oxford English Dictionary* under *Marmalade.*

III. ORANGE MARMALADE IN ENGLAND: THE BEGINNINGS

1. Sir K. Digby, *The Closet...Open'd, 1669,* ed. A. Macdonnell (1910), 243.
2. See p. 37.
3. This book was formerly ascribed to Elizabeth Grey, Countess of Kent, but Elizabeth David has shown in *Petits Propos Culinaires* 1 (1979), 43–53, that it is unlikely either to have belonged to the Countess or to have been used in her household.
4. La Varenne, *Cuisinier françois,* part 3, 42.
5. A selection of the recipes in her book was published in 1974. See Bibliography, under R. Price.
6. A. Boorde, *A Compendyous Regyment, or A Dyetary of Helth, 1542,* ed. F. J. Furnivall (Early English Text Society) (1870), 286.
7. Elyot, *Castel of Helth,* 27v.
8. See pp. 61f.
9. Henry Power memoranda, in British Library, MS Sloane 1351, 69v. I am indebted to Jennifer Stead for allowing me to use her transcript of this page.

IV. MARMALADE IN SCOTLAND: THE BEGINNINGS

1. See p. 40.
2. E. H. M. Cox, *A History of Gardening in Scotland* (1935), does not anywhere mention quince trees.

3. S. Tolkowsky, *Hesperides* (1938), 299–300.
4. According to the accounts in *The Household Book of Lady Grisell Baillie, 1692–1733,* ed. R. Scott-Moncrieff (1911).
5. T. C. Smout, 'The Early Scottish Sugar Houses, 1660–1720', *Economic History Review* 14 (1961–2), 241.
6. Tolkowsky,*Hesperides*, 267.
7. See p. 39.
8. W. Macintosh, of Borlum, *An Essay on Ways and Means for Inclosing, Fallowing, Planting . . . in Scotland* (Edinburgh, 1729), 230.
9. S. Johnson, *A Journey to the WesternIslands of Scotland,* ed. M. Lascelles (New Haven, 1971), 56.
10. J. Boswell, *Journal of a Tour to the Hebrides with Samuel Johnson, 1773,* ed. F. A. Pottle and C. H. Bennett (1963), 132, 134.
11. F. M. McNeill, *The Scots Kitchen* (2nd ed. 1963), 236.
12. Quoted by F. W. Hackwood, *Good Cheer* (1911), 275.

V. ORANGE MARMALADE: THE YEARS OF EXPANSION

1. I am indebted to Miss E. Greenwood of Chivers Hartley for drawing my attention to this advertisement.
2. J. Galt, *The Ayrshire Legatees, 1821,* ed. D. S. Meldrum, vol. 2 (1936), 96, 302.
3. A. H. Hassall, *Food and its Adulterations* (rev. ed. 1855), 516.
4. The details about the history and products of present-day marmalade manufacturers in this chapter and the next come from the records of the firms named. I am indebted to their representatives (see *Preface)* for supplying this information.
5. N. Deerr, *The History of Sugar,* vol. 2 (1949), 427–30, 441.
6. McNeill, *Scots Kitchen,* 235–6.

VI. HOME-MADE MARMALADE YESTERDAY AND TODAY

1. *Harmsworth's Household Encyclopaedia*, vol. 3 (1923), 2643 and illustration.
2. Tolkowsky, *Hesperides*, 216, 266–7.

VII. THE MARMALADE MARKET YESTERDAY AND TODAY

1. Hassall, *Food and its Adulterations,* 514.
2. A. H. Hassall, *Adulterations Detected* (1857), 415–16.

3. J. C. Jeaffreson, A *Book about the Table* (2nd ed. 1875), vol. 1, 218.
4. I am indebted to the representatives of the firms named in this chapter (see *Preface)* for the information concerning their products which is reproduced here.
5. See Chapter IV, above.
6. I am indebted to Mr Anthony Blunt for sending me, via Ms G. Sinclair, details of this event, together with the longer account of his first experiment in making liqueur marmalade which is quoted in full below.
7. The information is this and the next two paragraphs is derived from Henrietta Green, 'Pulp, peel and pots to fill', *The Independent*, 3 February 1990; and R.W. Broomfield, 'The manufacture of preserves...', in *Fruit Processing*, ed. D. Arthey and P.R. Ashurst, (London, 1996), 175–9.
8. T. N. Morris, *Principles of Fruit Preservation* (3rd ed. 1951), 145 note.
9. MINTEL, 'Sweet Spreads Report', *Market Intelligence Information* (April 1998).
10. Ibid.

VIII. TASTES IN MARMALADE YESTERDAY AND TODAY

1. Hassall, *Food and its Adulterations,* 514.
2. MINTEL, 'Sweet Spreads Report', (April 1998).
3. A. Davis, *Let's Eat Right to Keep Fit* (New American Library) (New York, 1970), 127–8.

IX. MARMALADE IN THE WIDER WORLD

1. I am indebted to William W. Weaver, of Devon, Pennsylvania, for sending me, via Alan Davidson, information about Cuba.
2. Tolkowsy, *Hesperides,* 258–9.
3. Josselyn, *Two Voyages,* 193.
4. *Martha Washington's Booke of Cookery and Booke of Sweetmeats,* transcribed with historical notes by K. Hess (New York, 1981), intro., 6.
5. See pp. 47ff.
6. Weaver, see above, ref. 1.
7. See p. 78.
8. Tolkowsky, *Hesperides,* 257.
9. M. Symons, *One Continuous Picnic* (Adelaide, 1982), 17–18, 39.
10. Ibid., 60, quoting W. Kelly, *Life in Victoria* (London, 1859).

11. I am indebted to Alan and Jane Davidson, Professor Constance B. Hieatt, Janet Hine, Helen Peacocke, Rosemary Suttill, and Beth Tupper, who have sent me information about marmalade's role in various parts of the world today.
12. Later renamed 'Select orange marmalade'.
13. Michael Davie in *The Observer* (22.1.84), 29.
14. Department of Agriculture, Victoria, bulletin 43 [Melbourne, 1930s?], 37–39.
15. B. Wood, ed., *Tucker in Australia* (Melbourne, 1977), 70.
16. McNeill, *Scots Kitchen*, 236.

COOKERY-BOOK
BIBLIOGRAPHY

The books listed here are the ones used in compiling the text of *The Book of Marmalade*. Place of publication is London, unless otherwise stated.

ABBOT, R., *The Housekeeper's Valuable Present*, [c.1800].

The Accomplished Ladies Rich Closet of Rarities, 7th ed. 1715.

ACCUM, F., *Culinary Chemistry*, 1821.

ACTON, E., *Modern Cookery in all its Branches*, 1845. Newly revised and much enlarged ed. 1855.

ALEXIS OF PIEDMONT (Girolamo Ruscelli), *The Secrets of . . . Alexis of Piedmont*, 1562.

BEETON, I., *The Book of Household Management*, 1861.

BORELLA, MR, *The Court and Country Confectioner*, 1770. New ed. 1772.

BOWMAN, A., *The New Cookery Book*, 2nd ed. 1869.

BYRON, M., *May Byron's Jam Book*, 1917.

Cassell's Dictionary of Cookery, [c. 1881].

Cassell's Domestic Dictionary, [c. 1884].

CASTLEHILL, LADY (Martha Lockhart), *Lady Castlehill's Receipt Book: a Selection . . . from a Collection made in 1712*; ed. with intro. by H. Whyte, Glasgow, 1976.

CLELAND, E., *A New and Easy Method of Cookery*, Edinburgh, 1759.

A Closet for Ladies and Gentlewomen, 1608.

COBBET, A., *The English Housekeeper*, 2nd ed. [c. 1840]. 3rd ed. 1842.

A Daily Exercise for Ladies and Gentlewomen, 1617.

DAWE, N.H., *The Wife's Help to Indian Cookery*, 1888.

DIGBY, SIR K., *The Closet Opened, 1669*, ed. A. Macdonnell, 1910.

DODS, M. (C. I. Johnstone), *The Cook and Housewife's Manual*, Edinburgh, 1826. 3rd ed., Edinburgh, 1828.

DUCKITT, H.I., *Hilda's 'Where is it?' of Recipes*, 2nd ed. 1891.

FARMER, F., *The Boston Cooking-School Cook Book*, Boston, Mass., 1899.

FRAZER, MRS, *The Practice of Cookery, Pastry, Pickling, Preserving . . . etc.*, London & Edinburgh, 1791.

GLASSE, H., *The Art of Cookery made Plain and Easy*, 1747. *The Compleat Confectioner*, [c. 1765].

[143]

Harmsworth's Household Encyclopaedia, vol. 3, 1923.

HUISH, R., *The Female's Friend, and General Domestic Adviser,* 1837.

KETTILBY, M., *A Collection of above Three Hundred Receipts in Cookery, Physick and Surgery,* 1714.

LEA, E.E., *Domestic Cookery,* 5th ed., Baltimore, 1853, reprinted as: *A Quaker Woman's Cookbook,* intro. W. W. Weaver, Philadelphia, 1982.

M., W., *The Queen's Closet Opened,* 1655.

MACIVER, S., *Cookery and Pastry,* 3rd ed., Edinburgh, 1782.

MCLINTOCK, MRS, *Receipts for Cookery and Pastrywork,* Glasgow, 1736.

MARKHAM, G., *The English Huswife,* 4th (enlarged) ed. 1631.

Martha Washington's Booke of Cookery and Booke of Sweetmeats, transcribed and annotated by K. Hess, New York, 1981.

MASON, C., *The Lady's Assistant,* 1775.

PARTRIDGE, J., *The Treasurie of Commodious Conceites, and Hidden Secrets,* 1584.

PEARSON, I., *Australian Cookery: Recipes for the People,* Melbourne, 1894.

PLAT, SIR H., *Delightes for Ladies,* 1605.

PRICE, R., *The Compleat Cook,* compiled [from MS] and intro. M. Masson, 1974.

RAFFALD, E., *The Experienced English Housekeeper,* Manchester, 1769.

ROBERTSON, H., *The Young Ladies School of Arts,* 4th ed., York, 1777.

RUNDELL, M.E., *A New System of Domestic Cookery,* 1806. 2nd (enlarged) ed. 1807.

RUTHVEN, LORD PATRICK, *The Ladies Cabinet Opened,* 1639; *The Ladies Cabinet Enlarged and Opened,* 1654.

SALMON, W., *The Family Dictionary,* 2nd ed. 1696.

SMITH, E., *The Compleat Housewife,* 1727.

STEER, F.A. & GARDINER, G., *The Complete Indian Housekeeper and Cook,* new and revised ed. 1909.

A True Gentlewoman's Delight [formerly ascribed to Elizabeth Grey, Countess of Kent], 1653.

The True Way of Preserving and Candying, 1681.

Victoria Department of Agriculture, Bulletin 43, Melbourne, [1930s?].

W., A., *A Book of Cookrye,* 1587.

WEBSTER, T., *An Encyclopaedia of Domestic Economy,* 1844.

The Whole Duty of a Woman, 1737.

WOOLLEY, H., *The Queen-like Closet,* 5th ed. 1684.

A Yorkshire Cookery Book, ed. M. M. Gaskell, Wakefield, 1916.

RECIPES

I. Historic Recipes

The recipes are numbered R 1, R 2, etc., and are referred to in the text by those numbers. The Greek, Latin and medieval French recipes have been translated, and the spelling of the English recipes has been modernised except in the case of headings, and of a few distinctive terms.

[R 1] *Mēlomeli*   *1st century* AD

Mēlomeli, which is also called *kudōnomeli*, is prepared from Cydonian apples [quinces] when the seeds have been taken out and the fruit thrust down into honey as hard as possible, so that it is wedged solid. It will become soft after a year, like wine-honey, and is suitable for the uses for which the latter is prepared.

Dioscorides, *De Materia Medica*, 5.21.

[R 2] *For Cydonites*   *4th century* AD

Having removed the skin from ripe Cydonian apples [quinces], cut them up into very small, fine shreds, and throw away the hard part inside [i.e. the core]. Then cook in honey until the pulp is reduced to half its measure, and as it cooks, sprinkle fine-ground pepper over it.

Another method. Two pints of quince juice, a half-pint of vinegar, two pints of honey: mix together and boil down until the whole mixture resembles the consistency of pure honey. Then take care to mix in two ounces of ground pepper and ginger.

Palladius, *Opus Agriculturae*, 11.20.

[R 3] *To make Condoignac*   c.*1394*

Take the quinces and peel them. Then divide into quarters, and discard the eye and the pips. Then cook them in good red wine, and then they are to be strained through a sieve. Then take honey, and boil it for a long time and remove the scum, and afterwards put your quinces into it and stir very well, and let it boil until the honey is reduced at least to half. Then throw into it hippocras powder [i.e. powdered spices, such as cinnamon, nutmeg, and ginger, used to flavour the spiced wine called 'hippocras'], and stir until it is quite cold. Then cut it into pieces and store them.

Le Ménagier de Paris, ed. G. E. Brereton & J. M. Ferrier (Oxford, 1981), 269.

[R 4] *Chardequynce*   c. *1444*

Chardecoynes that is good for the stomach is thus made: take a quart of clarified honey and 2 ounces of powder of pepper and meddle them together, and then take 20 quinces and 10 wardens [large pears] and pare them and take out the kernels with the cores and seeth them in clean [ale-]wort till they be tender and then stamp them in a mortar as small as thou mayest and then strain them through a strainer and that that will not [go] well through put in again and stamp it oft and oft drive it through a cloth or strainer, and if it be too dry put in half a saucerful or a little more [of wort?] for to get out the other the better and then put it to the honey and set it on the fire and make it to seeth well and stir fast with a great staff and if there be 2 stirrers it is the better for both: if it be [not] strongly stirred, it will set [stick] to the vessel and then it is lost; and seeth it till it [be] sodden thick and then take it down off the fire and when it is well nigh cold put in $^{1}/_{4}$ ounce of ginger and as much of canell [cinnamon] powdered and meddle them well together with a slice and then let it cool and put it in a box; this manner of making is good, and if it [is] thus made it will be black; if thou wilt make more at once, take more of each one after the proportions, as much as thou list.

Another manner of making and is better than the first: for to put in 2 parts of honey and 3 parts of sugar and then shall this be better than the other, and in all other things do as thou did before, for thou mayest well enough seeth thy quinces in water, and it is good enough though thou put no wort thereto, and if you wilt, thou mayest make it without wardens, but it is the better with wardens.

The third manner of making is this, and is the best of all, and that is for to take sugar and quinces alike much by weight, and no honey nor pears and in all other things do as thou didst before, and this shall be whiter than that other, inasmuch as the sugar is white [so] shall the chardequynce be.

A Leechbook, Royal Medical Society MS 136,
ed. W. R. Dawson (1934), 62–4, Nos. 156–8.

[R 5] *To make drie Marmalade of Peaches*　　　　　　　　*1587*
Take your peaches and pare them, and cut them from the stones, and mince them very finely, and steep them in rosewater, then strain them with rosewater through a coarse cloth or strainer into your pan that you will seeth it in: You must have to every pound of peaches half a pound of sugar finely beaten, and put it into your pan that you do boil it in: You must reserve out a good quantity to mould your cakes or prints withall of that sugar, then set your pan on the fire and stir it till it be thick or stiff that your stick will stand upright of itself, then take it up and lay it in a platter or charger in pretty lumps as big as you will have the moulds or prints, and when it is cold print it on a fair board with sugar: and print thereon a mould or what knot or fashion you will, and bake it in an earthen pot or pan upon the embers, or in a fair cover, and keep them continually by the fire to keep them dry.
Marmalade of Quinces or any other thing
Take the quinces and quarter them, and cut out the cores and pare them clean, and seeth them in fair water till they be very tender, then take them with rosewater and strain them, and do as is aforesaid in everything.　　　　　　　A.W., *A Book of Cookrye* (1587), 42

[R 6] *To make printed Quodiniacke of Quinces a Rubye Colour 1608*
Take two pounds of quinces, pared and cut in small pieces, and put
them into a posnet with three pints of fair water, and so let them boil
till they be tender, then put into them a pound of sugar, and let it boil,
till it come to his colour and thickness, then print it with your moulds,
you shall know when it is ready to print by rolling a little upon the back
of a spoon, and if you see that it will stand and not run down, print
it; in like sort you may make your quodiniacke of pippins, your pippins
will hold all the year.

A Closet for Ladies and Gentlewomen (1608), 46.

[R 7] *To make an excellent Marmelate which was given Queene Mary for
a New Yeare's Gift*   *16th century*
Take a pound and half of sugar, boil it with a pint of fair water till it
come to the height of Manus Christi [a sweetmeat], then take three
or four small quinces, one good orange peel, both very well preserved
and finely beaten, & 3 ounces of almonds blanched and beaten by
themselves; Eringus [sea-holly] roots preserved, two ounces and a half,
stir these with the sugar till it will not stick, and then at the last put in
of musk and amber [ambergris], dissolved in rosewater, of each four
grains, of cinnamon, ginger, cloves and mace, of each three drams, of
oil of cinnamon two drops, this being done put it into your Marmelate
boxes, and so present it to whom you please.

A Closet for Ladies and Gentlewomen (1608), 43.

[R 8] *To make another sort of Marmelate very comfortable and restorative to any Lord or Lady whatsoever*   *1608*
Take of the purest green ginger, six drams, of Eringus and Saterion
roots, of each an ounce and a half, beat these very finely, and draw them
with a silver spoon through a hair searse [sieve], take of nut kernels and
almonds blanched, of each an ounce, cocks stones half an ounce, all
steeped in honey twelve hours, and then boiled in milk and beaten and
mixed with the rest, then powder the seeds of red nettles or rocket, of

each one dram, plantain seeds half a dram, of the belly and back of a fish called Scincus marinus three drams, of diasaterion four ounces, of cantarides add a dram, beat these very finely and with the other powder mix it, and so with a pound of fine sugar dissolved in rosewater, and boiled to sugar again, mingle the powder and all the rest of the things, putting in leaf-gold six leaves, of pearl prepared two drams, oil of cinnamon six drops, and being thus done and well dried, put it up in your Marmelate boxes and gild it, and so use it at your pleasure.

A Closet for Ladies and Gentlewomen (1608), 44.

[R 9] *To make white jellied Marmalade of Quinces*
Later 17th century
Take your quinces and quoddle them tender, then take the juice of grated quinces and wet your sugar, which must be the weight of that quantity of quoddled quinces you do, and make a syrup, then put in your quinces sliced thin and boil it apace till it will jelly.

Brotherton Library, University of Leeds
MS 687, No. 78. Reproduced by permission of the Librarian.

[R 10] *To preserve Oranges after the Portugall fashion* 1605
Take oranges and core them on the side and lay them in water, then boil them in fair water till they be tender, shift them in the boiling to take away their bitterness, then take sugar & boil it to the height of syrup, as much as will cover them, and so put your oranges into it, and that will make them take sugar. If you have 24 oranges beat 8 of them till they come to paste, with a pound of fine sugar, then fill every one of the other oranges with the same, and so boil them again in your syrup: then there will be marmalade of oranges within your oranges, and it will cut like an hard egg.

Sir Hugh Plat, *Delightes for Ladies* (1605), A34.

[R 11] *To make Marmelade of Lemmons and Oranges* 1605
Take ten lemons or oranges and boil them with half a dozen pippins,

and so draw them through a strainer: then take so much sugar as the pulp doth weigh, and boil it as you do marmalade of quinces; and then box it up.

Sir Hugh Plat, *Delightes for Ladies* (1605), A41.

[R 12] *To make Pippin Marmalet*   *Later 17th century*
Take pippins & boil them a good while, then strain it, & to a pint of that water & a little more, put a pound of sugar, then slice candied orange peels & put them into the syrup, boil it very fast, & when it is almost enough, put in some juice of oranges & lemons, more or less according to your taste, after, boil it fast a little, and then glass it up, & if you like it you may put in s[ome am]ber [gris].

Martha Washington's Booke of Cookery and Booke of
Sweetmeats, ed. K. Hess (New York, 1981), 241, No. 27.

[R 13] *To make Lemon Marmelett*   *1683*
Pare your lemons very thin, cut them in the middle round ways, pick out the seeds & meat, & squeeze out the juice, put the rinds into water four days, shifting them twice a day, then boil them in 5 or 6 several waters. Let the water boil before you put them in, and when they are tender take them out, & when they are cold, pick out the strings, squeeze out the water clean from them, then take half a pound of lemon-rind & half a pound of pulp of pippin, beat them fine in a mortar, then R. [recipe = take] the weights, half the weight of good loaf sugar, & to every pound of pulp a pint of pippin-liquor, set the pulp, the sugar, & liquor aboiling, & when it is almost enough boiled, put in the meat & juice of the lemons. Thus you may do oranges.

MS Recipe Book of Margaret Savile of Methley, 1683,
Yorkshire Archaeological Society MS DD 148, No. 47.

[R 14] *To make Orange-Marmalade, very good*   *England, 1714*
Take eighteen fair large Sevil-oranges, pare them very thin, then cut them in halves, and save their juice in a clean vessel, and set it covered

in a cool place; put the half-oranges into water for one night, then boil them very tender, shifting the water 'till all the bitterness is out, then dry them well, and pick out the seeds and strings as nicely as you can; pound them very fine, and to every pound of pulp take a pound of double-refined sugar; boil your pulp and sugar almost to a candy-height: When this is ready, you must take the juice of six lemons, the juice of all the oranges, strain it, and take its full weight in double-refined sugar, and which pour into the pulp and sugar; and boil the whole pretty fast till it will jelly. Keep your classes covered, and 'twill be a lasting wholesome sweetmeat for any use.

M. Kettilby, *A Collection of above Three Hundred Receipts in Cookery, Physick and Surgery* (1714), 78.

[R 15] *To make Marmalet of Oranges and Lemons*   Scotland, 1736
Take oranges, grate them, and cut them through the middle, squeeze out the juice; take the pulp of the oranges, and beat it very well in a mortar, and put it through a search [sieve]; take the skins of the oranges and boil them till they be very tender, then beat them very fine, mix your juice, pulp and skins altogether, and for every pound of Marmalet, take a pound of fine sugar, mix the sugar and oranges together, set them on the fire, and when it comes to the boiling, put in the grate of the oranges, and let it boil till it cut easily with a knife, when cold, then take it off the fire, and pour it into your pots.

Mrs McLintock's Receipts for Cookery and Pastry-work (Glasgow, 1736), 24.
Reproduced from the copy in Glasgow University Library by permission of the Librarian.

[R 16] *To make Orange Marmalade*   Scotland, 1760s
To the largest best Seville oranges, take the same weight of single refined sugar; grate your oranges; then cut them in two, and squeeze out the juice; throw away the pulp; cut down the skins as thin as possible, about half an inch long; put a pint of water to a pound of sugar; make it into

a syrup; beat the whites of three or four eggs, and clarify it; put in your rinds and gratings, and boil it till it is clear and tender; then put in your juice, and boil it till it is of a proper thickness; when it is cold, put it in your pots, and paper it up; this is by much the easiest and best way of making marmalade.

H. Robertson, *The Young Ladies School of Arts,* 4th edition (York, 1777), 83. The 1st edition (1766) and the 2nd edition (1767) 'with large additions' were published at Edinburgh.

[R 17] *Transparent Marmalade*   *England, 1769*
Take very pale Seville oranges, cut them in quarters, take out the pulp, and put it into a bason, pick the skins and seeds out, put the peels in a little salt and water, let them stand all night, then boil them in a good quantity of spring water till they are tender, then cut them in very thin slices, and put them to the pulp, to every pound of marmalade put a pound and a half of double refined sugar beat fine, boil them together gently for twenty minutes; if it is not clear and transparent, boil it five or six minutes longer, keep stirring it gently all the time, and take care you do not break the slices: when it is cold, put it into jelly or sweetmeat glasses, tie them down with brandy papers over them. They are pretty for a dessert of any kind.

E. Raffald, *The Experienced English Housekeeper* (Manchester, 1769), 188.

[R 18] *Orange Marmalade*   *England, 1842*
Put 6 Seville oranges into a scale, and weigh their weight, and half their weight again, of lump sugar: to every lb. of fruit measure a wine-pint [16 oz. = American pint] of cold spring water. Cut the fruit in quarters, remove the pips and throw them into the water; then cut the oranges in slices on plates, so as not to lose any part of the juice or pulp, then take the pips out of the water, put all the fruit, juice, and sugar in, and boil it gently an hour, or until it is sufficiently consistent. Put by in pots.

A. Cobbett, *The English Housekeeper,* 3rd edition (1842), 313.

[R 19] *Lemon Marmalade*   *North America, 1845*
Soak the peel of lemons that have been left after making lemonade, changing the water twice a day for three days to extract the bitter; boil them till soft, then mash and put in enough sugar to make it pleasant to the taste; stew it a short time after the sugar is put in; put it in a bowl, and when cold, cut it in slices for the table; it will keep several weeks.

E. Ellicott Lea, *Domestic Cookery*,
5th edition (Baltimore, 1853), 139–40.

[R 20] *Lemon Marmalade (Níbú Murabbá)*   *India, 1888*
Cut up the lemons very finely, removing all the seed. To every half-seer [1 seer = 2 lb. English weight] allow three pints of water, and soak for twenty-four hours. Boil till quite tender, then let them stand for a day. Allow three-quarters of a seer [1 $^1/_2$ lb.] of sugar to each half-seer [1 lb.] of fruits, and boil till it will set.

Orange (Nárangí) marmalade is made by following the above recipe. [N.B. This would be sweet orange marmalade; Seville oranges (Kuttas) are mentioned in some other recipes for use in India.]

N. H. Dawe, *The Wife's Help to Indian Cookery* (1888), 678.

[R 21] *Grated Marmalade*   *Australia, 1888*
20 oranges, bitter; 1 lemon; 1 gill of water; 1 lb. of sugar to 1 lb. of fruit.
Mode. Grate the rind of the oranges and lemon, then scoop out the inside and remove seeds, bruise the pulp with a very little water, and press through a sieve. Weigh the pulped oranges and allow 1 lb. of sugar to 1 lb. of fruit, place this into preserving pan, add the gratings and boil till the rind is tender.
Note. When grating the oranges and lemon, throw the grated rinds into cold water, strain through piece of muslin when wanted.

J. Pearson, *Australian Cookery: Recipes for the People,
as given at the Centennial Exhibition, Melbourne,
1888–1889* (Melbourne, 1894), 110.

2. Marmalade Recipes for Today

A few reminders
The fruit should be well scrubbed. Nowadays it is possible to speed marmalade preparation by cutting the peel with the slicing attachment of an electric food mixer. The time spent on the first stage (the boiling of the peel or whole fruit) can be reduced by using a pressure cooker. Pressure-cooking time for citrus peels or fruits is usually about 15 minutes, and the pan should then be left closed for at least 10 more minutes to complete cooking and allow pressure to drop. For the second stage, use the pan without its lid. Conversely, a pressure-cooker recipe can be used in conjunction with an ordinary preserving pan, provided that the citrus peels or fruit are simmered more slowly until they reach the required degree of softness before they are reboiled with sugar, juices, etc. at the second stage. Where lemon-juice is added to improve the set, citric or tartaric acid may be used as a substitute ($^1/_4$ teaspoon = 1 tablespoon lemon-juice; $^1/_2$ teaspoon = juice of an average lemon). Many people believe that cane sugar inverts more easily than beet sugar, and is less likely to recrystallise when the marmalade is stored for a long period. Test cooked marmalade on a cold saucer (chill in refrigerator); if the surface of the cooled marmalade crinkles when pressed with a finger, then it is ready. Cool before potting.

Family marmalade
3 lb. (1.4 kg.) Seville oranges; 6 lb. (2.8 kg.) sugar; juice of 2 lemons; 5 pints (2.8 litres) water. Soak oranges for 3 minutes in hot water, then take off peel. Squeeze the juice from the hearts and cut up pulp. Finely slice peel, and put pips into muslin bag. Put juice, pulp, peel into pan together with water and bag of pips, and cook gently until the peel is tender (about 2 hours). Press out pectin from bag of pips over pan with the backs of two spoons, and discard bag. Stir sugar and lemon juice into contents of pan, and boil rapidly until setting point is reached (15–25 minutes). Yield: about 10 lb. (4–5 kg.).

Special thick marmalade, pressure cooked
2 lb. (0.9 kg.) Seville oranges; 3 lb. (1.4 kg.) sugar; 3 pints (1.7 litres) water. Scrub fruit and put into pressure cooker whole with $^1/_4$ pint (1.4 dcl.) of the water. Cook under pressure for 15–20 minutes, and allow pressure to drop gradually. Lift fruit into colander to cool a little. Scoop out the middles (integuments and pips) and simmer in small pan with $^3/_4$ pint (4.3 dcl.) more of the water for at least 10 minutes to extract pectin; sieve, pressing out all the liquid, keep liquid and discard integuments and pips. Meanwhile, slice the rinds as thick or fine as you want, add to the two cooking liquids with the remaining water, and reheat in open pan. Add sugar and boil until setting point is reached.

This marmalade is nearly all 'chunk' and of very intense flavour. If you prefer more jelly, add $^1/_2$ pint (2.8 dcl.) or more of water, and $^1/_2$ lb. (225 gm.) or more of sugar. Both ways are very good.

To make dark marmalade, add 1 level tablespoon of black treacle at the end of the final boiling time.

J.S.

Orange jelly marmalade
Take 9 Seville oranges, two sweet oranges, and 2 lemons; cut them across in thin slices, put the pips aside, and cover the fruit with 9 pints (5.1 litres) of water. Let this stand for 24 hours. Next day put it into a preserving-pan, add the pips tied in a muslin bag, and boil gently for about an hour, or until it has been reduced by half. Strain through a jelly-bag or clean cloth and allow to drip overnight. Measure the juice, to each pint (6 dcl.) allow a pound (450 gm.) of preserving-sugar, and boil together until it will set. Pour into sterilised jars, and cover when cold.

F. M. McNeill, *The Book of Breakfasts,* 1932.

Marmalade for puddings (uncooked)
Boil 12 Seville oranges till they are quite tender, changing the water two or three times; take out the seeds, pulp and inner skin of the rind;

beat the outer rind in a mortar to a fine paste, add to it the pulp and juice; to every pound of this, add two pounds of fine, moist sugar; mix the whole well together; put it into a larger jar than will hold it, to admit of fermentation. It will thus keep for years, and ready to be used for puddings, when other materials are scarce.

Dictionary of Daily Wants, vol. 2 [1860].

'Compost-heap marmalade'

Make this when there is a glut of garden apples, and the flesh has been turned into apple-sauce, etc. to store (the cores and skins and the orange-peels are the 'compost'). It requires: the peels of 6 sweet oranges; 1 pint (6 dcl.) of apple-pectin (made from a preserving pan full of peels and cores – or use windfall apples – boiled down with water to a pint); 2 lb. (0.9 kg.) sugar; 3 teaspoons citric acid. Cook orange-peels in apple pectin until tender, then cut into slices or chunks and replace in pectin. Dissolve the sugar and citric acid in the pectin, and boil until setting point is reached (about 10 mins.).

J.S.

Lemon marmalade

2 lb. (0.9 kg.) lemons; 4 lb. (1.8 kg.) sugar; 4 pints (2.2 litres) water. Wash fruit. Squeeze out juice and reserve. Scoop out pulp and cut up peel. Soak peel and pulp overnight in the water, together with the pips tied up in a piece of cheesecloth or muslin. Next day simmer peel and pulp slowly in the same water, together with the bag of pips, in a covered pan. When peels are soft (about 1 $^1/_2$ hours), remove pips, stir in warmed sugar and add lemon-juice. Bring to the boil with pan uncovered, and boil rapidly until setting point is reached (about 20 minutes).

Beaten lemon marmalade, modern style

1 lb. (450 gm.) lemons; 1 pint (6 dcl.) water; sugar. Weigh a large jug. Squeeze juice from lemons and reserve. Roughly cut up juiced lemons,

put pieces into preserving pan with water and simmer until peel is soft (1–1 $^1/_2$ hours), topping up with water if necessary. Put contents of pan through blender; then weigh in jug. Deduct weight of jug to calculate actual weight of pulp, and weigh out an equal quantity of sugar. Return pulp to pan, and add sugar and the reserved lemon juice. Bring to boil, and boil rapidly until setting point is reached (10–15 minutes). Yield: 3 $^1/_4$–3 $^1/_2$ lb. This marmalade can also be made with Seville oranges. Include one lemon to 2 lb. oranges, to ensure a good set.

Old Southern lemon jelly [US]
The juice and grated rind of 4 lemons; 1 lb. (450 gm.) sugar. Stir until sugar is partly dissolved. Cook over slow heat, stirring constantly until it thickens. Remove from heat, cool and seal in a glass jar.

Grapefruit marmalade [New Zealand]
4 large grapefruit; 2 lemons; 12 breakfast-cups water; 12 breakfast-cups sugar. Slice grapefruit and lemons very finely; cover with water and leave overnight. Next day, boil for 20 minutes; add sugar; bring quickly back to the boil, and boil for 30 minutes. Test for setting.

B.T.

Grapefruit jelly marmalade
2 lb. 2 oz. (1 kg.) grapefruit; 1 orange and 1 lemon (total weight 1 lb. = 450 gm.); 6 pints (3.4 litres) water; sugar. Wash fruit, and remove peel very thinly. Cut peel into fine strips, and tie in a piece of muslin. Cut remaining fruit and pith into pieces, and place in preserving-pan with the water. Simmer 2 hours. Simmer bag of peel in water to cover for 1 $^1/_2$ hours or more. Remove peel and reserve. Pour cooking-water into pulp mixture. Pour contents of pan into jelly-bag and strain overnight. Measure juice, bring to boil and add 1 lb. (450 gm.) sugar to every 1 pint (6 dcl.) juice. Add acid if required, and add reserved peel. Cook to setting-point.

Pink grapefruit and ginger marmalade
2 pink grapefruit; 2 large lemons; 3 lb. (1.4 kg.) sugar; 4 pints (2.3 litres) water; 4 oz. (125 gm.) crystallised ginger. Peel the grapefruit and lemons with a serrated knife. Mince the peel. Remove the pips and tie in a piece of muslin. Chop the pulp and put into a preserving pan together with the minced peel. Add 4 pints (2.3 litres) water and the muslin bag of pips. Boil slowly until the peel is soft and the liquid has reduced to half the original quantity ($1^1/_2 - 2$ hours). Squeeze the bag of pips over the pan between the backs of two spoons to extract the pectin; then discard the bag. Chop the ginger and add to the contents of the pan, and stir in the warmed sugar. Then boil rapidly until the setting point is reached (15–25 minutes). Cool to blood-heat, stir well, and pot up. Yield: about 5 lb.

Tangerine jelly marmalade
2 lb. (0.9 kg.) tangerines or mandarins; 2 medium lemons; 1 grapefruit; $4^1/_2$ pints (2.5 litres) water; $3^1/_2$ lb. (1.6 kg.) sugar. Cut tangerine-peel very finely and simmer with 1 pint (6 dcl.) of water for $1^1/_2 - 2$ hours until tender. Squeeze lemons and reserve juice. Roughly cut lemon-peel and pulp, grapefruit peel and flesh and tangerine flesh, add $2^1/_2$ pints (1.4 litres) of water and pips in cheesecloth bag, bring to boil and simmer for about 2 hours. Strain through jelly-bag. Return pulp to pan, add remaining water, cook for 15–20 minutes and strain through jelly-bag. Combine the 2 strained liquids and the lemon-juice, add the sugar, and heat until it dissolves. Add the cooked, shredded tangerine peel, and boil hard to setting point.

Cumquat marmalade [Australia]
Slice the cumquats, remove their seeds, cover them with water and leave overnight. Next morning, boil gently for one hour; turn out into bowl and leave for 24 hours. Measure and add $1^1/_2$ lb. (675 gm.) sugar to every 1 lb. (450 gm.) of pulp. Boil gently for about three-quarters of an hour, and test for setting.

Lime marmalade

8 limes; sugar; water. Wash limes. Place in preserving-pan with enough water to cover them and boil gently until soft (1 $\frac{1}{2}$– 2 hours); or pressure-cook for 15 minutes under pressure, and then reduce pressure gradually (10–15 minutes). Slice limes finely, remove pips and weigh the fruit. For each 1 lb. (450 gm.) fruit, allow 1 lb. (450 gm.) sugar and 1 pint (6 dcl.) water. Boil together in open pan to setting point (20–30 minutes). Cool before potting.

Honeydew-lime marmalade

2 limes; $\frac{1}{2}$ honeydew melon; 1 $\frac{1}{2}$ lb. (675 gm.) sugar; $\frac{1}{2}$ pint (3 dcl.) water. Quarter the limes and pressure-cook in the water at 15 lb. pressure for 15–20 minutes. Cool for 10 minutes, remove limes and slice thinly. Cut melon into small dice (if unripe, simmer for a short time). Combine fruit, add sugar, and cook in open pan to setting-point.

J.S.

Redcar marmalade

4 Jaffa oranges; 4 lemons; 1 grapefruit; 4 pints (2.3 litres) water; sugar. Wash the fruit, put it in the water and boil for 15 minutes. Cut the fruit in halves, remove the seeds and put through the mincer. Put the pulp into the water in which the fruit was boiled; then measure. To every cupful of pulp and liquid put a cupful of sugar, and boil for 45 minutes, when it will jelly nicely.

P. Hutchinson, *Old English Cookery,* 1973.

Three-fruit marmalade, pressure cooked

1 large grapefruit; 1 large orange; 1 lemon; juice and pips of another lemon; 2 lb. (0.9 kg.) sugar. Cut grapefruit, lemon and orange in halves. Place them in pressure cooker with one pint (6 dcl.) water. Cook under 15 lb. pressure for 10 minutes. Cool. Open pressure cooker and check that fruit is tender; then chop into chunks. Collect all pips and place in a piece of muslin or net. Measure water in pressure cooker, and

make up to 1 pint (6 dcl.) again. Put all back into cooker and add sugar. Do not put lid on again, but boil in open pan until the marmalade sets (15–20 minutes).

Gold jelly [US]
2 grapefruits; 2 oranges; 2 lemons; sugar; water. Shred or chop fruit fine, after removing all seeds and fibres. Measure and cover with three times its volume of water. Let stand until next day; then boil 3 minutes, and let stand till next day. Measure (in cupfuls), and add equal amount (cupfuls) of sugar, and boil until it jellies.

L. P. Harden, *The Southern Cookbook,* 1951.

Orange walnut marmalade [US]
1 grapefruit; 3 sweet oranges; $2^{1}/_{2}$ pints (1.4 litres) water; $2^{1}/_{2}$ lb. (1.2 kg.) sugar; $^{1}/_{4}$ lb. (115 gm.) coarsely-chopped walnuts. Wash fruit; quarter and remove seeds and pulp. Cut peel in thin strips; add pulp, water and sugar. Leave to stand overnight. Boil slowly, stirring occasionally, about $1^{1}/_{2}$ hours, or until mixture is thick and peel is tender. Add chopped walnuts. Pour into hot, sterilised jars, filling to top, and cover at once.

Orange pineapple marmalade
3 Jaffa oranges; 1 lemon; 1 large tin pineapple; 4 lb. (1.8 kg.) sugar; 1 pint (6 dcl.) water. Wash and peel oranges and lemon. Shred peel finely and cut up all the fruit into small cubes. Cover with pineapple juice and one pint (6 dcl.) water, and leave overnight. Simmer in preserving pan until tender. Add sugar and boil to setting point (30–40 minutes). Put in warmed glass jars, and seal when cool.

GALOP (Grapefruit, Apple, Lemon, Orange, Pineapple) marmalade [Australia]
1 grapefruit; 1 apple; 1 lemon; 1 orange; 1 pineapple; water; sugar. Skin the citrus fruit. Cut up orange, lemon and grapefruit peel and soak in

water to cover overnight. Next day cut up apple, pineapple and pulp of orange, lemon and grapefruit. Allow a cup of water to each cup of fruit and peel, using the water in which the peel has soaked and adding extra water if necessary. Bring to boil in preserving-pan and cook till tender (about 1 hour). Measure, and to each cup of the mixture allow a cup of sugar. Dissolve the sugar in the mixture, and boil rapidly until it will set.

Lemon, watermelon and ginger marmalade [Fiji]
1 pink-fleshed watermelon (3–4 lb.; 1.4–1.8 kg.); 2 lemons; 3 lb. (1.4 kg.) sugar; 1 tablespoon minced root ginger. Cut up the melon flesh into cubes, reserving the pips. Peel off the lemon-peel taking as little pith as possible, and cut the peel into neat shreds. Squeeze out the lemon-juice and reserve. Heat the melon cubes gently until the juice begins to run, then add the lemon shreds, and put into the pan a muslin bag containing the melon and lemon pips, the minced ginger and the inner peel and flesh of the lemons, roughly cut up. Cook gently for about half an hour. Put in the sugar and lemon-juice, and boil rapidly to setting point.

R.S.

Lemon and tomato marmalade [US]
5 lb. (2.25 kg.) firm, ripe tomatoes; 2 fresh lemons; 2 teaspoons grated ginger root; 4 lb. (1.8 kg.) preserving-sugar. Peel and slice tomatoes; cut lemons in paper-thin slices; add grated ginger-root. Simmer gently for an hour. Add sugar and cook until thick and smooth, stirring towards the end so that it does not stick. Cool. Pour into jelly-glasses and seal. Served with cooked meats, and 'always a prime favourite with the men-folk'.

Orange and peach marmalade
4 lb. (1.8 kg.) peaches (small, slightly unripe ones are best); 3 large oranges; 2 pints (1.1 litres) water; preserving sugar. Peel the orange rind

thinly and cut into strips. Cover these with boiling water and leave overnight. Remove white pith and pips and cut up the oranges; peel and cut up peaches and put into preserving pan with orange-peel and water. Simmer gently for 1 hour, then add equal weight of sugar. Boil together until thick.

Quince marmalade

4 lb. (1.8 kg.) quinces; 2 lemons; 5 lb. (2.25 kg.) sugar; 3 $^{1}/_{2}$ pints (2 litres) water. Peel and core the quinces and cut into cubes. Grate the skins of the washed lemons, and add gratings, if liked. Simmer quinces in water until tender (20–35 minutes). Then add lemon-juice and sugar, and boil fast to setting point.

Japonica marmalade

1 lb. (450 gm.) japonica fruit, unpeeled; 1 pint (6 dcl.) water; the juice of 1 lemon; sugar. Cut fruit in halves, but do not peel or core. Simmer in the water until they turn to pulp. Sieve, measure, and add a cupful of sugar for each cupful of pulp. Add lemon-juice, stir till sugar is dissolved, and then boil to setting-point.

3. MARMALADE COOKERY FOR TODAY

MEAT COOKERY

Beef casserole

1 $^{1}/_{4}$ lb. (575 gm.) braising steak; 2 tablespoons orange marmalade; 1 dessertspoon wine-vinegar; $^{1}/_{2}$ teaspoon cinnamon; $^{1}/_{2}$ teaspoon powdered coriander; $^{1}/_{4}$ teaspoon nutmeg; 1 clove garlic, finely sliced; salt; 6 prunes; olive oil. Cut the meat into 1 inch (2.5 cm.) cubes and brown in the oil. Place in a casserole dish, or in a heavy saucepan, and lay the prunes on top. Melt the marmalade in 6 tablespoons of warm water, and stir in the vinegar and seasonings. Pour the liquid into the dish or pan so that it just covers the meat, adding a little extra water if necessary. Cook casserole in a moderate oven, 180°C (350°F), gas mark 4, for

three-quarters of an hour, or until the liquid comes to the boil; then reduce heat to 140°C (275°F), gas mark 1, and cook for about 2 $^1/_2$ hours, or until the meat is tender. Or, bring saucepan to the boil, then simmer for 2 $^1/_2$ – 3 hours.

Pork casserole

1 $^1/_2$ lb. (675 gm.) fillet/leg-steak of pork, trimmed and divided into portions; 2 tablespoons orange marmalade; 1 dessertspoon wine-vinegar; $^1/_2$ teaspoon powdered coriander; $^1/_4$ teaspoon nutmeg; 1 clove garlic, finely sliced; salt; grated peel of 1 orange; 1 cooking apple; olive oil. Lightly brown the pork in the oil, and arrange the pieces in a casserole dish. Melt the marmalade in 6 tablespoons of warm water, and stir in the vinegar, seasonings and grated orange-peel; then pour over the pork pieces. Slice the apple, and lay the slices over the meat. Cover the casserole, and cook in a moderate oven, 180°C (350°F), gas mark 4, for three-quarters of an hour, then reduce heat to 140°C (275°F), gas mark 1, and cook for a further hour, or until pork is tender.

Marinated grilled chicken

'Ruth's grilled chicken in lime marinade' is the name of a dish served at Morton's Restaurant in Beverley Hills. The meat of a young and juicy bird is marinated for a day in lime marmalade, with garlic and soy sauce, and is then broiled over charcoal; when served it is 'permeated with the lovely perfume and taste of lime'. (*Gourmet*, Vol. 41, No. 1, January 1981.) The following is an adaptation that can be cooked under the kitchen grill:

2 chicken breasts, boned, trimmed and divided to make 4 portions; 3 tablespoons lime marmalade; 2 teaspoons soy sauce, *or* 1 $^1/_2$ teaspoons wine-vinegar and $^1/_2$ teaspoon turmeric; 1 clove garlic, finely chopped; $^1/_2$ teaspoon salt; olive oil. Warm the marmalade with 2 or 3 teaspoons of water until it begins to melt, stir in the seasonings (but not the olive oil), and leave to cool. Then spread thickly over each side of the chicken portions; on the skin side, slit and lift the

skin here and there, and insert some of the marinade. Arrange chicken in a glass or china bowl, pour over any remaining marinade, cover, and leave in a cool place for 8–12 hours, turning the pieces once or twice during that time. Heat grill, and line grill-pan with foil. Then remove chicken from marinade, and pat the pieces dry with kitchen paper. Brush them lightly with olive oil, and grill them. If a sauce is desired, add $^1/_2$ pint chicken stock to the remaining marinade, bring to the boil and simmer for 10 minutes.

Glazed gammon

2–3 lb. (0.9–1.4 kg.) corner gammon; 3–4 tablespoons coarse-cut orange marmalade; 2 tablespoons soft brown sugar; 1 teaspoon of made mustard. Gammon may be pre-soaked for 24 hours in 2 or 3 changes of water, wrapped in foil, placed on a grid in a baking-tin half-filled with water, and baked at 170°C (325°F), gas mark 3, until nearly done. Alternatively, it may be boiled: bring it to the boil, just covered in water, in a saucepan; change the water once, and bring it back to the boil, then simmer for $1\,^1/_2 - 2$ hours, until nearly done. *To glaze.* Peel off the rind, mix the marmalade, sugar and mustard well together, and spread and press down over the fatty surface of the gammon. Stand it on a grid over a clean (or rinsed-out) baking-tin, and bake for 20–30 minutes, basting frequently.

Glaze for roast duck

Use ginger marmalade as part of the glaze for a roast duck.

C.B.H.

Marmalade as a relish

Marmalade may be served with roast pork, duck, or goose, and with hot, boiled ham.

F. M. McNeill, *The Scots Kitchen,* 2nd edition 1963.

SAUCES

Marmalade sherry sauce
Take two large tablespoons of orange marmalade, put it into a saucepan with a wineglassful of sherry, another of water, and six lumps of white sugar. Boil until the sugar is dissolved, and thicken with arrowroot (or cornflour). Sufficient for a large pudding. Time to make, about 5 minutes. Probable cost, *10d.*

Cassell's Dictionary of Cookery, [c. 1881].

A modern economical version: 2 tablespoons marmalade; 6 table-spoons hot water; 1 dessertspoon sherry or brandy. Dissolve the marmalade in the water, add the sherry or brandy, and heat, but do not boil.

Marmalade lemon sauce
4–6 tablespoons marmalade; 2 tablespoons lemon-juice, and grated lemon-rind, if liked; 1 teaspoon cornflour; 6 tablespoons water. Blend the cornflour with the lemon-juice. Boil the water with the grated lemon-rind, and slowly add the dissolved cornflour, stirring all the time. Boil for 5 minutes, then add the marmalade, stir and bring back to the boil.

Runny marmalade sauce
1 tablespoon marmalade; 1 tablespoon golden syrup; 1 dessertspoonful lemon-juice; $^1/_4$ pint (1.5 dcl.) water. Put all ingredients together into a saucepan, and bring slowly to the boil, stirring now and then.

Plombière sauce [US]
6 tablespoons orange marmalade; 2 tablespoons water; 4 tablespoons toasted coconut. Put the marmalade and the water into a saucepan, warm and stir together. Add the coconut. Serve with ice-cream.

Orange-cumquat sauce

2 tablespoons orange marmalade; 2 tablespoons crushed pineapple; 3 tablespoons sliced cumquats; 1 oz. (30 gm.) crystallised ginger, finely shredded; 4 tablespoons crushed tinned mandarin oranges; 4 tablespoons mandarin syrup; 1 teaspoon cornflour. Mix the cornflour with a very little water, and combine with the mandarin syrup. Pour into a saucepan, add all the other ingredients, and stir together while bringing slowly to the boil. Simmer for 5 minutes. Serve with ice-cream. Especially good to follow a Chinese meal.

J.S.

Marmalade cinnamon sauce

2 ripe eating pears; 6 oz. (175 gm.) orange marmalade; $^1/_2$ teaspoon cinnamon; 1 oz. (30 gm.) candied peel, shredded; 1 oz. (30 gm.) crystallised ginger, finely shredded. Peel and dice pears, and cook in a very little water for 10 minutes. Add all the other ingredients, and slowly reheat, stirring them together. Simmer for a further five minutes. Serve with ice-cream.

Orange marmalade syrup for pancakes [Canada]

$^3/_4$ cup orange marmalade; $^3/_4$ cup water; 2 tablespoons butter. Melt marmalade in water over low heat, and cook until smooth. Stir in butter. Serve warm.

Relish for honeydew melon

When serving honeydew melon, remove pips from interior, divide melon into slices, and spread the inside surface of each with ginger marmalade.

PUDDINGS AND DESSERTS

Snowdon pudding

4 oz. (115 gm.) stoned raisins; 3 tablespoons cornflour; 8 oz. (230 gm.) shredded suet; 8 oz. (230 gm.) fresh white breadcrumbs; pinch salt; 6 oz.

(175 gm.) lemon marmalade; 6 oz. (175 gm.) soft brown sugar; 6 eggs; the grated rind of 2 lemons; a little butter. Butter a 2 $^1/_2$ pint (1.5 litre) basin, and press the raisins to the butter across the bottom and around the sides. Mix together the cornflour, suet, breadcrumbs, salt, lemon-rind, marmalade and sugar. Beat the eggs and combine with the other ingredients, blending them together into a smooth mixture. Fill the basin; cover with a well-buttered square of foil, making a 1 inch (2.5 cm.) pleat across the middle, to allow for expansion, and tie it down firmly with fine string. Steam in a two-tier steamer or a saucepan half-filled with water for 1 $^1/_2$ hours. Enough for 8 servings. Eliza Acton added the recipe for this pudding to the enlarged edition of her *Modern Cookery* in 1855. Her own comments were: 'Half the quantity given above will fill a mould or basin which will contain rather more than a pint, and will be sufficiently boiled in 10 minutes less than an hour. To many tastes, a slight diminution in the proportion of the suet would be an improvement to the pudding . . . This pudding is constantly served to travellers at the hotel at the foot of the mountain from which it takes its name.'

Marmalade queen pudding
1 pint (6 dcl.) milk; grated rind of 1 lemon; 4 oz. (115 gm.) breadcrumbs; 2 oz. (60 gm.) butter; 4 oz. (115 gm.) caster sugar; 3 eggs, separated; 3 tablespoons orange marmalade. Put the breadcrumbs into a bowl. Warm the milk gently, together with the grated lemon-rind, in a saucepan. Stir in the butter and 2 oz. (60 gm.) of the sugar. Pour the liquid over the breadcrumbs, cover the bowl, and leave for 10 minutes. Beat up the egg yolks and stir into the bread mixture. Turn it into a buttered fireproof dish, and bake at 180°C (350°F), gas mark 4, for 15 minutes or until lightly set. Warm the marmalade, and spread over the bread-custard. Whisk the egg-whites until stiff, gradually beating in the remaining sugar. Pile on top of the pudding, and return it to the oven for a further 10–15 minutes, until the meringue is crisp and slightly brown.

Marmalade and vermicelli pudding

1 breakfastcupful of vermicelli; 2 tablespoonfuls of marmalade; $^1/_4$ lb. (115 gm.) of raisins; sugar to taste; 3 eggs; milk. Pour some boiling milk on the vermicelli, and let it remain covered for 10 minutes; then mix with it the marmalade, stoned raisins, sugar and beaten eggs. Stir all well together, put the mixture into a buttered mould, boil for 1 $^1/_2$ hours, and serve with custard sauce.

I. Beeton, *The Book of Household Management*, 1861.

Christmas pudding

Replace part of the sugar in your favourite Christmas pudding recipe with marmalade. For each 1 oz. (30 gm.) of sugar omitted, add 1 tablespoon of marmalade and 1 tablespoon of breadcrumbs.

Apple and almond tart

Pastry: 6 oz. (175 gm.) plain flour; $^1/_4$ teaspoon salt; 3 oz. (85 gm.) butter; $^1/_2$ oz. (15 gm.) sugar; 1 egg yolk. *Filling*: 1 $^1/_4$ lb. (575 gm.) cooking apples; juice of half a lemon; 1 tablespoon dried breadcrumbs; 4 tablespoons orange or lemon marmalade; 1 oz. (30 gm.) flaked almonds. Sift flour and salt into a mixing-bowl; flake butter and rub in. Combine sugar and egg yolk and stir in to form a stiff dough. Cool in refrigerator. Mix the lemon-juice with a tablespoon of water. Wash and cut up the apples, but do not peel or core them. Dip the pieces in the lemon water, and put into a saucepan, adding any remaining lemon water; cook gently until soft. Work the cooked apples through a sieve, mix the pulp with the marmalade and leave to cool. Roll out pastry, and use most of it to line a 8-inch (23 cm.) flan tin. Prick the base and sprinkle with breadcrumbs. Fill with the apple mixture. Roll the remaining pastry into thin strips and make a lattice over the top. Bake in preheated oven at 200°C (400°F), gas mark 6, until pastry is golden-brown (20–25 minutes). Remove flan from oven, and sprinkle the surface with flaked almonds.

Orange and almond tart

8 oz. (225 gm.) shortcrust pastry; 3 tablespoons orange marmalade; 2 large oranges; 3 oz. (85 gm.) ground almonds; 4 oz. (115 gm.) sugar; 1 egg, separated. Line two 7-inch (18 cm.) flan tins with the pastry, and spread marmalade over the base of each. Peel the oranges and cut into thin slices, removing white pith and pips. Divide the slices, and lay over the marmalade in each flan tin. Mix the almonds with the sugar, and beat in the egg yolk. Whisk the egg white until stiff, and fold into the almond mixture. Spread half over one flan filling, and half over the other. Bake in hot oven, 220°C (425°F), gas mark 7, for 10 minutes, then reduce heat to 150°C (300°F), gas mark 2, for about 30 minutes more. Serve hot or cold.

Sutton pie

1 ¹/₂ lb. (675 gm.) cooking apples; juice of half a lemon; 3 tablespoons orange marmalade; 8 oz. (225 gm.) self-raising flour; 4 oz. (115 gm.) butter or margarine; 2 oz. (60 gm.) brown moist sugar; 2 oz. (60 g.) rolled oats. Cut up apples, dip in lemon-juice mixed with a tablespoon of water, cook and sieve (as in *Apple and almond tart* recipe above); and combine the apple-pulp with the marmalade. Mix flour and sugar, and rub in butter. Take half of this mixture, divide it again and press into the bases of each of two shallow 8-inch (20 cm.) pie dishes. Take 1 oz. (30 gm.) of the oats, divide and sprinkle over each dish. Cover with apple puree. Sprinkle over the remaining oats and then the rest of the crumble. Bake for 30–40 minutes at 190°C (375°F), gas mark 5.

Spicy rhubarb and marmalade crumble

1 ¹/₄ lb. (575 gm.) rhubarb, approximately; 3 tablespoons orange or lemon marmalade; 3 oz. (85 gm.) flour; 3 oz. (85 gm.) brown sugar; 2 oz. (60 gm.) butter; pinch salt; ¹/₂ teaspoon cinnamon; ¹/₂ teaspoon ginger. Wash rhubarb and cut into one-inch lengths. Put it into a pie-dish, and spoon the marmalade over it. Sprinkle with ¹/₄ teaspoon cinnamon and ¹/₄ teaspoon ginger. Sift together the flour, sugar, salt

and $^1/_4$ teaspoon each of cinnamon and ginger. Work together with the butter until the mixture becomes crumbly; then spread it over the rhubarb and marmalade. Bake in a hot oven, 200°C (400°F), gas mark 6, for about half an hour, until fruit is cooked and top is browned.

Mincepies

As a change from the usual mincepies, try filling the pie-cases with a mixture of mincemeat and marmalade (a spoonful to a spoonful, in equal quantities). Cover with pastry lids with slits in them, as the mixture is moister than mincemeat alone. Pies with this filling keep well.

Marmalade bavarian

1 tangerine jelly; $^1/_4$ teaspoon salt; 5 oz./ $^1/_4$ pint (150 gm./1.5 dcl.) cream; 2 tablespoons orange marmalade. Make up jelly with 1 $^3/_4$ cups/ $^7/_8$ pint (5 dcl.) hot water and the salt. Chill until syrupy. Then whip the cream until thick but not too stiff, and fold in. Then fold in the orange marmalade. Pour into mould and chill. Unmould, and garnish with cream and marmalade. Serves 6.

J.S.

Orange marmalade whip

5 egg whites; small pinch of salt; $^1/_4$ lb. (115 gm.) granulated sugar; 3 tablespoons orange marmalade; 1 teaspoon curaçao. Beat egg whites and salt until stiff, and beat in sugar very slowly. Then beat in marmalade and curaçao. Pour into a well-greased 1 quart (1.1 litre) deep baking-dish, set it in a pan of water, and bake at 140°C (275°F), gas mark 1, for one hour. Unmould, and serve warm, not hot, with marmalade sherry sauce.

Marmalade trifle

Your usual trifle recipe can be the basis for a marmalade trifle. The day before it is to be made, measure out the sherry or brandy which is to moisten the trifle sponge/macaroons/ratafias, but replace one table-spoon of it with the juice of half an orange (Seville or sweet, as preferred), or half a lemon. Carefully take the zest from the orange or lemon peel, and leave it to soak overnight in the alcohol and fruit-juice mixture. Next day remove the zest, and use the liquid to moisten the base layer of the trifle. Replace the usual covering layer of raspberry or apricot jam with a layer of marmalade. Add the custard layer. Finally, beat a little curaçao or other orange liqueur into the whipped cream which is to crown the trifle, and decorate it with split blanched almonds and orange or lemon shreds (to make these, take some new pieces of zest from the peel of half an orange or half a lemon, bring to the boil in $^1/_4$ pint (1.5 dcl.) water, and simmer for 2 minutes to remove bitterness; then cut into fine shreds).

Marmalade ice cream
1 pint (6 dcl.) single cream; 2 egg yolks; 4 oz. (115 gm.) caster sugar; $^1/_2$ lb. (225 gm.) coarse-cut marmalade; $^1/_4$ pint (1.5 dcl.) whipped cream. In one saucepan combine the egg yolks with the sugar, and have a second, larger saucepan ready, partly filled with boiling water (or use the 2 parts of a double boiler). In a third saucepan, bring the single cream just to the boil. Pour it over the egg mixture, whisking well, and let it cook over the simmering hot water, stirring constantly, until it thickens to custard consistency. Remove from heat, and stir in the marmalade, previously warmed so that it is runny. Allow the mixture to cool, and then fold in the whipped cream. Freeze at a very low temperature, stirring 2 or 3 times during the process to ensure an even texture.

CAKES

Marmalade walnut cake
6 oz. (175 gm.) butter; 6 oz. (175 gm.) caster sugar; grated rind of 1 orange; 2 eggs, separated; 2 heaped tablespoons marmalade; 2 oz. (60 gm.) finely chopped candied peel; 3 oz. (85 gm.) chopped walnuts; 5 tablespoons water; 10 oz. (275 gm.) self raising flour. Cream the butter

and sugar together, adding the orange-rind. Beat in the egg yolks. Stir in the marmalade, nuts and peel, then the water and the flour. Finally, fold in the stiffly-beaten egg whites. Bake in a preheated oven at 180°C (350°F), gas mark 4, for about 1 ¼ hours (test with a skewer, which will come out clean when it is done). Keeps well.

M.L.

Marmalade raisin cake

7 oz. (200 gm.) plain flour; 1 teaspoon baking powder; pinch salt; 5 oz. (150 gm.) butter or margarine; 3 oz. (85 gm.) sugar; 2 eggs; 4 tablespoons marmalade; 6 oz. (175 gm.) seedless raisins; 2 tablespoons milk. Grease and line a 7-inch (18 cm.) round cake tin. Combine the flour, baking powder and salt. In another bowl, cream the butter with the sugar. Beat the eggs and stir them in, together with the marmalade, fruit and milk. Finally, fold in the flour, and transfer to cake tin. Bake in a preheated oven at 180°C (350°F), gas mark 4, for about 1 ¼ hours.

Coconut cake [Cumberland]

4 oz. (115 gm.) sugar; 6 oz. (175 gm.) margarine; 4 tablespoons marmalade; 3 eggs; 6 oz. (175 gm.) self raising flour; 2 oz. (60 gm.) desiccated coconut. Cream the sugar and margarine thoroughly, and stir in the marmalade. Beat the eggs and add gradually. Fold in the flour and coconut, and blend well. Put into 2 greased 7-inch (18 cm.) sandwich tins, and bake until firm at 180°C (375°F), gas mark 5. When cool, sandwich together with marmalade.

J. Poulson, *Old Northern Recipes,* 1975.

Chocolate cake

4 oz. (115 gm.) butter; 3 oz. (85 gm.) sugar; 1 tablespoon marmalade; 2 oz. (60 gm.) Chocolat Menier; 2 tablespoons drinking chocolate; 3 oz. (85 gm.) ground almonds; 2 large eggs; 4–6 tablespoons self raising flour. Cream together butter and sugar. Beat in marmalade, Chocolat Menier (previously melted over low heat), drinking chocolate and

almonds. Whisk eggs and add, together with 2 tablespoons of flour. Fold in as much more flour as is needed to bring to a soft cake consistency. Transfer to a 7-inch (18 cm.) greased and lined cake tin, and bake in a slow oven at 170°C (340°F), gas mark 3, for about 1 hour 20 minutes.

Marmalade ring
8 oz. (225 gm.) self raising flour; pinch salt; 3 oz. (85 gm.) margarine; 1 tablespoon caster sugar; 1 egg, lightly beaten and made up to ¼ pint (1.5 dcl.) with milk; 3 tablespoons coarse-cut orange marmalade; 2 oz. (60 gm.) sultanas; 2 oz. (60 gm.) granulated sugar. Grease and flour a baking sheet. Sift flour with salt, and rub in margarine. Stir in sugar. Mix in egg with milk, and knead gently to make a soft dough. Roll out into a flat piece about 8 inches by 12 inches (20 cm. x 30 cm.). Spread with marmalade and sultanas, leaving ½ inch (1.5 cm.) clear round all edges. Roll it up, starting at one of the longer sides. Make cuts through outer layer of pastry at top of roll at one inch intervals, and then bend round to form a ring, joining up the ends, and lay on prepared baking sheet. Bake in centre of preheated oven at 200°C (400°F), gas mark 6, for 25 minutes. Make a glaze by dissolving the granulated sugar with 3 tablespoons of water over low heat; simmer for 2 minutes. Remove marmalade ring from oven when ready, and brush glaze over it immediately.

Viennese tarts
4 oz. (115 gm.) butter; 2 oz. (60 gm.) icing sugar; 2 oz. (60 gm.) plain flour; 2 oz. (60 gm.) cornflour; ginger marmalade; lime marmalade. Cream together butter and sieved icing sugar. Mix in flour and cornflour. Roll into small balls, and press into greased tartlet tins, so that each forms a tartlet shape. Bake in a preheated moderate oven at 180°C (350°F), gas mark 4, for about 45 minutes, until pale golden and very firm. When cool, remove from tins and fill half of them with ginger marmalade, and the other half with lime marmalade.

Orange marmalade muffins [US]

2 oz. (60 gm.) butter or margarine; 2 oz. (60 gm.) sugar; 2 eggs; 7 oz. (200 gm.) plain flour; 2 teaspoons baking powder; $^1/_2$ teaspoon salt; $^1/_4$ pint (1.5 dcl.) milk; orange marmalade. Cream together butter and sugar; beat eggs and stir in. Sift together flour, baking powder and salt; add alternately with milk to creamed mixture. Then divide the mixture. Use half to fill greased patty tins $^1/_3$ full; place one teaspoon of marmalade in each section; cover with remaining mixture, so that each section is just over $^2/_3$ full. Bake in hot oven, 200°C (400°F), gas mark 6, for 15–20 minutes. Serve warm.

SANDWICHES

Marmalade can add an extra dimension to a wide variety of sandwich fillings.

The following are some ideas for closed sandwiches:

1. Orange marmalade and grated cheddar cheese.
2. Ginger marmalade and cream cheese.
3. Orange marmalade and peanut butter.
4. Orange marmalade and sliced bananas.
5. Orange or lemon marmalade with fresh mint leaves.
6. Lime marmalade with fresh parsley sprigs.
7. Orange marmalade with a covering of chopped soft lettuce leaves ('All the year round' variety) and chopped walnuts. Add another layer of marmalade to the upper slice of bread to help hold the sandwich together.

GENERAL INDEX